So You Want to be in Youth Ministry?

A guide on what to know before jumping in

Shawn M. Catalano

Cover design by Janine Dueck

Copyright © 2015 Shawn M. Catalano.

All rights reserved. No part of this book may be used or reproduced by any means, graphic, electronic, or mechanical, including photocopying, recording, taping or by any information storage retrieval system without the written permission of the author except in the case of brief quotations embodied in critical articles and reviews.

Scripture quotations are from The Holy Bible, English Standard Version® (ESV®), copyright © 2001 by Crossway, a publishing ministry of Good News Publishers. Used by permission. All rights reserved.

WestBow Press books may be ordered through booksellers or by contacting:

WestBow Press
A Division of Thomas Nelson & Zondervan
1663 Liberty Drive
Bloomington, IN 47403
www.westbowpress.com
1 (866) 928-1240

Because of the dynamic nature of the Internet, any web addresses or links contained in this book may have changed since publication and may no longer be valid. The views expressed in this work are solely those of the author and do not necessarily reflect the views of the publisher, and the publisher hereby disclaims any responsibility for them.

Any people depicted in stock imagery provided by Thinkstock are models, and such images are being used for illustrative purposes only.
Certain stock imagery © Thinkstock.

ISBN: 978-1-5127-0556-0 (sc)
ISBN: 978-1-5127-0557-7 (hc)
ISBN: 978-1-5127-0555-3 (e)

Library of Congress Control Number: 2015912157

Print information available on the last page.

WestBow Press rev. date: 04/06/2016

Contents

Introduction vii

Chapter 1: Why This Ministry? 1

Chapter 2: Major, Minor, or Nothing? 10

Chapter 3: Trying to Be Cool ... When We're Not 23

Chapter 4: Questions, Questions, Questions 31

Chapter 5: Big Church v. Small Church 37

Chapter 6: Leadership 101 51

Chapter 7: Time Management 67

Chapter 8: The Weekend Date 79

Chapter 9: Now that You've Arrived! 100

Conclusion 113

This book is dedicated to my wife Christine, and my four awesome kids – Tanna, Kylie, Brandon, and Zoey. Without all of you, this book never happens!

Introduction

Eighteen is a special number for anyone with a child. I remember by eighteen months old, each of my kids were walking and talking little people with their own personalities and attitudes. At that age my kids and I started to develop a new type of relationship. We would have conversations (as much as we could), and we would go on dates among others things. From the day a couple finds out they're pregnant to eighteen months later, life changes dramatically! We've gone from an excited, possibly frightened young couple to parents of a little person who is beginning to develop his or her own personhood. Those are huge changes!

Eighteen is a special number for any teenager. They all wait for this number from the beginning of high school. They assume that since that's the legal age of an adult, then life becomes so much easier afterward, that all of their teenage angst is over. They look at eighteen as the time when they're "mature enough to make their own choices" or when they're old enough to move out on their own. For parents, it can be a scary number because that's when our children become adults. It can remind us that they're about to hit the stage of life that will begin to solidify their future identities, careers, and life paths.

Unfortunately the number eighteen doesn't always hold a positive connotation in youth ministry. There are many stats out there that suggest that a lot of youth pastors only stay in a position for a maximum of eighteen months! That's a year and a half! That's heartbreaking! I'm sure for some there are staffing reasons for the change—promotion, role changes, leadership restructuring. However, I've met some who dropped out because they didn't feel ready. They came with their toolboxes full of ideas and plans, but they based all those plans on an event-driven ministry instead of a long-term discipleship-building ministry.

I've been blessed to have been involved in student ministry for more than twenty years, and each day I find joy and excitement in this ministry. It's not an easy ministry. But even my worst day in student ministry is still incredibly better than most people's best days in their careers. It's allowed me to hang on when others decided it was time to move on. And when a youth leader or pastor moves on, the church goes on. The church will find another person to fill that role, another staff member to own the ministry. They'll find someone to do retreats, teach the Bible, and prepare reports and budgets. But the church isn't really the one who usually gets damaged.

Think of the students.

In a teen's world, trust is huge. They so badly want someone in their lives they can trust, someone who will believe in them. The culture we currently live in treats teenagers like they're lesser humans, like they're only good for manual labor but have nothing else to offer the world. They hear it from the media, many of their teachers and coaches, and everywhere they turn. If we as youth ministers want to truly change the world and impact the lives of teens, we have to be in it for the long run. Leaving after eighteen months isn't the core of the issue. It's a symptom of something worse. It's a symptom that many of us don't see students as a mission field but as a stepping stone to another ministry. Our churches don't see teenagers as the church of today, just the church of the future, after the current leadership is gone. They don't invest in them other than providing a few token events. Many degree programs may be missing the target when it comes to training up and coming youth ministers. Teachers may spend more time on how to host retreats, games, or events instead of how to actually pastor students through difficult times. I always shutter when I attend conferences where there will be multiple seminars on hot games and crowd breakers but very few on counseling students through addiction or identity issues or on conflict management with parents and staff. My concern is that our young ministers are coming into their jobs with only eighteen months of plans in their toolboxes, and when those run out, they move on.

    This book has been in my heart for almost ten years. Over those ten years, I've met dozen of men and women who felt called to student ministry, and within three years of their first positions, they not only leave their churches but withdraw from ministry completely. I can't help but feel bad for them. Many of them have bachelor's and master's degrees, and they're changing oil at Walmart or working at a local fast-food place. They have a mountain of debt for a degree that they don't want to even use now. They're damaged because their calling is not there. For some their faith is weakened and damaged. Churches are suffering because they're spending a great amount of time and resources with a constant change in this ministry. When parents see that kind of constant change in the ministry where they have the most concerns for their children, we'll likely scare them off. They'll find a place where stability exists. Most of all, the students suffer. Just as they begin to trust a person, that minister moves on. After that happens more than once, those students tend to stop trying, stop attending, and stop following Jesus.

This book isn't meant to criticize anyone or anything. It's my way of trying to figure out how we reverse the eighteen-month trend. Imagine where our churches would be in ten to fifteen years if the national average went from eighteen months to five or six years? In my opinion that's the only way to motivate this generation to impact our world for Christ in unprecedented ways.

I always reference a verse in the song "Hosanna." The verse says, "I see a generation, rising up to take their place, with selfless faith." That's my goal for student ministry and more importantly, for student ministers. Let's show this culture of teens that we're in this for the long run with them. Good, bad, or ugly—we're sticking it out with them so that when they arrive in adulthood, they can look back and see that in addition to Jesus Christ, they had other adults with them for those formative years. They can point to other people who dedicated themselves to a ministry that changed lives. Then our prayer is that they'll turn around and do that for others. That's discipleship! We can do this!

Let's do it together!

Chapter 1

Why This Ministry?

Anyone who feels led into ministry with teens needs to ask him or herself one important question—*why?* What is it about working with students that is appealing? It's a thankless role that requires a lot of time, a lot of emotional investment, and a lot of patience. It can take a toll on our energy and minds. It requires that we keep different hours than others, taking late-night calls, responding to e-mails and texts on our days off, and much more. It's a ministry that requires a lot of investment.

I believe people need to ask why before they enter this ministry because it's not for the faint of heart. I've met many who have started in student ministry but have not lasted long because they didn't ask this question. Why is it so important? It's important because we need to commit with our eyes wide open. Proverbs 22:6 (ESV) says to "train up a child in the way he should go; even when he is old he will not depart from it." We can't do that in one year, and we can't do that halfheartedly.

I often wonder if many don't see longevity in this ministry because they buy into some false beliefs about student ministry. Let's debunk a few of those.

Myth #1: "You get to play with kids? How nice!"

Many times I've almost lost my patience with those who have made this claim. Don't get me wrong. Student ministry is and should be lots of fun! It's fun because you're ministering to people with lots of energy and creativity. You're serving a generation that desperately wants others to invest in and believe in them. They want to have fun with you, but they want so much more.

I'm not blaming people who think that. The simple fact is that there are many ministries that portray this myth! This isn't a judgment but an observation. Many youth ministries out there are based on games and activities. What many adults don't realize is that those students can be just as passionate about their faith as any adult can. However, many just see teenagers as physical laborers, helpers, but not much more than that. And that's a huge mistake. If we don't invest in our students, our churches will die. Plain and simple.

Be prepared for this statement, but don't let it bring you down. Use it as motivation to prove that statement wrong. Let your ministry show that we're not just "playing with kids."

Myth #2: "Kids just want to have fun. They're not really old enough to go deeper."

This is one of my major pet peeves within student ministry. As I read message boards online or hear other youth ministers talk, I'm shocked at the obsession with games. It seems like every Wednesday afternoon, I read or hear hundreds of leaders asking, "What game are you playing tonight or this weekend?"

That infuriates me! We tell students that God has a plan for their lives, and then we shove stupid games in their faces. I'm all for games and fun as a supporting element, but many student ministries make this their core with a devotional sprinkled in to "talk about Jesus." As you can probably tell, I'm very passionate about this.

Years ago I heard a quote that has stuck with me. Duffy Robbins, a popular youth ministry author and speaker, shared this on a couple of occasions. He said, "What you win people with is what you win them to." If we win students with games, prizes, and entertainment, that's what we'll win them to. That will be the expectation that becomes the norm. But if we can win them with the gospel, win them by helping them see the Bible as a living narrative instead of an old book, then we'll win them to something eternal!

Myth #3: "Our church doesn't *really* need a youth ministry."

If you're pursuing a career in student ministry, you'll undoubtedly come across this statement. In my experience it's not a statement meant to demean student ministry. It usually comes from someone who just hasn't seen what this type of ministry can mean to a local church. As someone who has been in student ministry for more than twenty years, I can tell you that it's absolutely vital. Many people in churches will fight to fund and staff our children's ministries but won't give a second thought to a student ministry. I currently serve as a kids and student pastor, so I can see the value of both. If we take this route, then we're only training our children till they reach the fifth or sixth grade, and then they're on their own. I believe churches that do this probably have a high attendance by people older than sixty but not many young families in the pews. We cannot drop kids when they hit their teenage years. That's the key time to invest in them because that's the time of life when they will form their identities for the rest of their lives.

Titus 2 exhorts adults to live in ways that will set the example for the next generation in order to "show yourself in all respects to be a good model of good works, and in your teaching show integrity, dignity, and sound speech that cannot be condemned" (Titus 2:7–8 ESV). It also commands that those who are older to "teach what is good" (Titus 2:3 ESV). Psalm 145:4 also tells us that "one generation shall commend your works to another, and shall declare your mighty acts." Why would we cut these off from our teenagers?

Myth #4: "I'll be a youth pastor until a senior pastor position opens up."

Before I go on, let me say that I am so appreciative of my lead pastor and the role he plays in our church. We are currently a multi-campus church, so I know his plate is ridiculously full. I respect anyone who fills that role in the church regardless of size. It takes high visibility and also high responsibility, and only a special person can fill that role. I say that because I don't want what I'm about to say to come across as anything against lead or senior pastors.

Let me say this as lovingly as possible: *If you are thinking about using student ministry as a stepping stone, don't!* I completely understand that many of us in youth ministry will make the transition to another role in our churches at some point. I know that God will call many of us to the role of lead/senior pastor as we mature and develop in our faith and pastoral abilities. I know that as much as I love being a student pastor, there will probably come a day when the Lord will lead me to a different ministry. When He does, I pray that I'll go willingly (although I'll be sad to say good-bye to student ministry). But that is much different than going into a role of youth pastor knowing that it isn't the ultimate goal.

I met a young man some time ago who shared with me that he felt led to be a lead pastor. He had a tremendous pastoral heart for people, loved the Word and its teachings, and was a great guy to spend time with. I got to spend a couple of months talking and interacting with him, and it was a blessing. During one lunch conversation, we were talking about my heart for students, and I was sharing what God had done in me to bring me where I was. As we talked, he mentioned that he might want to do some ministry with students. I was excited! Then he said the words I never like to hear. He said, "I think I'll look for a youth pastor position until a lead pastor position opens up. It will be fun." So do you know what I did?

I punched him!

No, not really, but that would really spice up the book, wouldn't it? But it opened up a terrific dialogue about his heart. I shared with him my concern with his statement. He'd gain the trust of students who desperately needed mentoring and love, but they would know the whole time that he could bail any day. I asked him, "If you took a youth pastor role on January 1 and a church offered you a lead pastor role on April 1, what would you do?" He said he'd probably take the lead pastor one since that's what he is "called to do." I tried to help him see that he would be walking away from students he was trying to invest in after only three months and show him the damage that could do to them.

I was thankful that he understood what I was saying, and actually up to this point, he hasn't pursued a youth pastor role. He's been serving faithfully on a church staff, and while he helps speak to students from time to time, he clearly understands his calling.

If you are thinking of working with students until another role opens up, I would ask you to rethink your approach. If you take a student pastor role, please pray about being all in. Students need adults who know what their calling is and need to see those adults jumping all-in to do it. They don't need another person in their lives "hanging out" with them till something better comes along. While your heart may not see it that way, they will.

Myth #5: "If eighteen months is the average, student ministry isn't a stable career."

I'm not going to lie. There is some truth to this. But I believe the instability isn't the result of the calculated national average of eighteen months. I believe it's because many are simply not ready when they go into the ministry. I'm not the perfect pastor. My students will verify that. I don't say that with self-defeat but as the truth. We're all fallen humans. Pastors are not the exception. But I will say this: I've been at my current role for more than eight years. I have friends who have been at their current churches for even longer. Stability is achievable! It comes not from gimmicks, music style, or how many Ping-Pong tables you have in your youth room. It comes from leaders like you and me dedicating ourselves to the ministry to teenagers and sticking it out through everything that comes with it.

Will parents always like you? Nope! However, for every parent who complains that their kid isn't getting enough attention, that you're not playing enough with the students, or that they think you charge too much for retreats and events, there are several who will hug you and thank you. They'll thank you for not giving up on their teens, whose behavior has stunk for the past few months. They'll thank you when they see their teens spending time in God's Word because we've challenged them to follow Jesus on their own and not just at church. They'll thank you because when their students had crises and they didn't talk to their parents, you reached out and helped. It *will* happen!

Will the people in your church always like and/or understand you and the ministry? Nope! I'll guarantee this will happen. Please remind yourself that it's not personal. It took me a lot of bumps, bruises, and damaged relationships to understand this. People won't feel this way because of who you are but more because of the unknown. In many churches, the youth ministry only shows itself during fundraisers, workdays, or testimonies during a "youth service." The rest of the year, the youth ministry stays in its room, works on its own schedule, and does its own thing. Don't let this happen. I can't stress enough how important it is to get your students involved in the church overall—serving, working in worship teams or parking teams, teaching in children's ministry, wherever they are gifted! Let the church see students as part of the church. When they do, they'll see that the students aren't the church of tomorrow. They're actually the church of today, and they're a vital part of the church moving forward. I've found that the more people see the students and the fruit in their lives from following Jesus personally, the more support the student ministry gets. We've seen this work at our church, and I can tell you without a doubt that our *entire* church supports our student ministry. They don't always get everything we do, but they see the fruit and trust our leadership.

Will you ever have conflict? Yep! Sometimes more than you want! Take a step back. Breathe. The world isn't out to get you. However, we're dealing with an age group that experiences many emotional ups and downs. They make and react to assumptions, and their attitudes can fly off of the handle—and that's just the parents! They're trusting us to lead, invest in, teach, and love their most precious gifts—their children. If we don't take that seriously, we will have conflict. And it's not because we're bad people. It's because a parent's investment and love in a student will always outweigh ours! We get the student for a few years. They invest in them for a lifetime. When conflict with parents comes up, before you respond, understand where they are coming from. Doing so will help both sides understand and communicate. Admit where you were in the wrong (even if it's not a big deal to you), and commit (not promise) to making the necessary changes. This doesn't mean you won't run into conflict with parents for reasons that are completely false or that don't involve you at all. It just means by hearing them out, it will be easy to discern what is legitimate and what may be an emotional complaint.

What about conflict with leaders? Do youth ministers ever have conflict with other church leaders? Of course! You know why? Because we are all leaders, and we all will have different ways of looking at things! And it's okay! Similar to dealing with parents, if conflict with a church leader rises up, take a step back and see where you may have been in the wrong. Once you identify that, go over and beyond to make it right. You may have to swallow your pride, and it can be uncomfortable! Is it healthy for you and that leadership relationship? Absolutely! We cannot have healthy staff relationships without conflict and healthy resolutions. If you feel a leader conflict is unfair or personal and the other side isn't willing to talk, take it to a direct supervisor, but do so with the heart to make amends and restore the trust and relationship, never to win an argument.

Our lead pastor (where I currently serve) has a document called "plumb lines." He gives them to all of the staff members, elders, deacons, and ministry leaders. He gave them to us under the instruction that "if we ever wonder what he thinks on certain issues, the plumb lines will help explain it to us." They're awesome and very helpful! He has a few on conflict, and they're ones that I try to hold to as best as I can. (However, I'm not always perfect at them.) He tells us to "display humility, grace, and patience in response and tone when we are confronted and/or challenged by anyone (even if wrongly challenged)." Conflict happens. It's part of ministry, but it doesn't have to destroy it.

These are a few myths that young ministers need to conquer to break the eighteen-month cycle.

Chapter 2

Major, Minor, or Nothing?

In my twenty years of serving with students, one of the questions I am asked the most is this: "If I'm going to be a youth pastor, does that mean I should get a youth ministry degree?"

I always give them the simplest, quickest answer I can. I simply say no.

This may not be a revelation for you, but I cannot count the number of college-age students I have spoken to who wrestle with this issue. They even make their college choices based on this information. While it's certainly not wrong to pursue a degree in youth ministry, it's definitely not the only way. As someone who has a bachelor's degree in youth ministry, I'm even beginning to wonder if earning the degree is even worth it.

Let me explain.

I absolutely loved my college experience. I had the privilege of attending a small Christian college in New York. I made lifelong friends there, friends I still see and spend time with on a regular basis. I really enjoyed my professors and learned a lot from them. I pursued a degree in youth ministry once I knew that this was the ministry God was leading me to. It was a great department and taught me a great deal. If I had to make one small criticism, it would be this: When I graduated, I wasn't prepared to be a youth pastor.

Please know that I am not blaming anything on my teachers, advisors, leaders, or college. And it wasn't that I didn't work hard. It's that I had no idea what to study or what to pursue. I had no idea where to go with my classes. I didn't really understand anything. I had adults in my life who guided, advised, and challenged me. However, I couldn't be them. I couldn't do ministry like them. I had to find how God wanted me to do ministry, and that wasn't something I learned in school.

As I continually think about the constant turnover in youth ministry, I can't help but wonder if we're not preparing young student pastors well enough in school. Are we helping them find God's call? Are we helping them understand that this ministry isn't about fifth-quarter events, Chubby Bunny tournaments, or lock-ins? Are we helping them see that they're accepting roles that will change the lives of hundreds of teens?

If I had the chance to go back to college, knowing what I know now, and could redo college, I wouldn't have chosen a youth ministry degree. I have nothing against it, but I would have chosen another degree path.

Many of my ministry classes involved reading several books, writing papers, and then taking a short final. I remember the classes being very interactive with lots of discussions and fun. But they were just about that. Many of the things we learned weren't helpful to me once I arrived in a full-time position. I learned a lot from the books they gave us but no more than if I had just ordered the books myself and read on my own. I know how ill prepared I felt after graduation, and I believe the teen culture was simpler then.

Today I speak to college students (at various schools) who feel like they're in the same boat. They're taking their time, resources, and efforts and putting them into learning things that may be outdated before they get to really use them. We're teaching techniques, not methods.

I fear that as leaders today, we're not doing a solid job or training up our replacements. Each of us in our current roles as youth leaders and pastors knows that the clock is ticking. No matter how much we don't want to admit it, there will come a time when youth ministry may not be our role—at least not as a hands-on minister. It's our God-given calling as pastors and ministers to raise up those coming behind us. It's harder when there are programs out there spending more time training young leaders and pastors in the hottest game ideas instead of discipleship methods. Some schools are giving out degrees in camping and retreat ministries or sports ministries instead of Bible teaching and pastoral methods degrees. While none of the former are evil and they don't mean that those people don't love Jesus or students, I have yet to see any student grow deeper in their faith by playing gaga ball.

So what should I do?

If I advised young men or women on their college decisions and they felt called into full-time student ministries, here are some majors I'd suggest:

Counseling/Psychology

In my twenty-plus years of serving in student ministry, one thing I've realized is that students are more concerned with the relationship they have with you than they are with how well you speak. Don't get me wrong. Anyone in this role needs to be able to handle the Word and communicate it clearly. That should be one of the top three characteristics that churches look at when they are hiring student pastors/directors. But in all my years, I've never had a student come up to me and say that exegetical exposition of the third chapter of the book of Matthew had changed his or her life. However, I've had many who have come up to me and shared that because I have listened and spoken to them, they've grown in their faith. What I learned from my psychology classes and counseling classes helped me do that. It helped me understand the mind and emotions of a teenager. It helped me learn solid listening and communication techniques. Most of all, it helped me learn my limits and know when to dig deeper and when to seek help in certain situations.

As I sit and write this chapter, I realize that about 40 percent of my normal workweek is dealing with students in counseling/pastoral care situations. As the current teen culture changes, it's my opinion that we will need to hone our counseling skills more and more.

Here's another thing we should always keep in mind as we pursue roles in student ministry: You may have the title of youth pastor or youth director, but you need to realize very quickly that you are ministering to the whole family. It's impossible to talk with students about their addiction issues without delving into how those issues are impacting their parents, their siblings, and their households. Nothing is ever simply a personal issue. The ripple effect can reach further than we see, and the issue may do more damage than we'll ever know. If we can equip ourselves to both understand the inner workings of the teen mind and psyche and also help guide them toward Jesus through those inner workings, we have a real chance of helping them overcome many of their issues. If we can serve a family in the same way, we can have an even greater impact.

Getting a specialization in biblical counseling can help one take techniques and strategically work Scripture into them. This can certainly help minister to students as well as the rest of the church.

A Secondary Education Degree

For some who are reading this book, the skills I mentioned previously come so naturally that you could be teaching some of those courses yourself instead of taking them. Either because of gifting or previous training, this is an area where you feel completely confident. Maybe the teaching piece is an area of need? Education degrees can help you with your technique, room control and management, and even some creative teaching methods.

I have never taken an education course, but if you were thinking of pursuing an education degree, I would suggest focusing on a secondary education degree. A secondary education degree focuses mostly on the middle school, high school, and some college-age students—the exact level of students we are potentially seeking to help. In those classes you'll learn a lot about how to teach a middle school or high school student. Most likely you'll learn how to do that teaching in a classroom setting. I'm of the mind-set that we should avoid a classroom setting or terminology in our ministries, but the techniques can be of great value to you. This program will help you to understand the learning style and abilities of most students in this age range. You can swap out the math, science, or history for the Scriptures and still accomplish your ministry goals. Education degrees can give you a lot of tools to help you in your ministry.

Another advantage of getting an education degree, especially a secondary education degree, is that it can open up so many other doors for you to minister in your local community. As the times have changed, schools have begun to tighten up security on their campuses. When I first came to the ministry, I was able to go have lunch with my students at their schools. It gave me a chance to see them in their school environments and meet their school friends, and for twenty to thirty minutes, I was able to show them I was interested in their lives outside of church. Where I serve now (in New York), those options aren't there. Schools here tend not to let visitors in unless they're on official business. So that eliminates one option I used to have. If you were to pursue a secondary education degree, you could gain access to schools as a substitute teacher or even as a full-time teacher. It can create incredible opportunities to minister in different ways. While it might be true that you cannot share the gospel openly as a teacher in some public schools, there is no rule against being another caring adult in a student's life or being the type of teacher who is willing to go the extra mile in helping a student succeed. Those can be ways to open new doors to the gospel. Please keep in mind that ministering to teens isn't always a full-time vocational job. It can happen in many different ways.

Pastoral Methods

This degree is probably named a dozen different things, depending on the school you attend. A degree in pastoral methods will help you get some training on the skills you will need to actually be a pastor. Whether you are male or female and regardless of the denomination you serve with, the skills in these classes can be valuable for anyone in ministry. They teach you what the role of a pastor really entails, the pitfalls and victories, and the traps to watch out for. The teachers go over sermon prep, leadership structures, choosing leadership roles, interacting with boards, etc. They cover all things that anyone in ministry could benefit from. A pastor I once served under used to tell us that he wished seminaries had a class called churchology. He envisioned it as a class where young ministers would hear the realities of pastoral ministry. We all agree that it's hard to learn everything in the classroom. Since the teachers in those rooms may not be involved in ministry any longer, the information can seem outdated. Pastoral methods can help you learn the *skeletons* of ministry. Experience will help you put meat on those skeletons.

Of course, to pursue student ministry, we shouldn't focus on just degrees. Training can happen in many different ways. Being successful in youth ministry doesn't hinge on our education or degree. Ultimately it hinges on our love for Jesus and our love for students. We can find resources to assist us.

For example, I love going to conferences! One of my favorite is the National Youth Workers Convention by Youth Specialties. Over the years I've enjoyed worshipping with the likes of David Crowder, Chris Tomlin, Starfield, and others. It's been great hearing speakers like Doug Fields, Francis Chan, Kendra Creasy Dean, and other prominent voices in youth ministry. I've been blessed by being able to sit in seminars and having chances to interact with other youth leaders/pastors from around the country. When you go to these conferences (and there are more than just the NYWC), you are reminded that there is a kinship between youth workers and also that you're part of a bigger movement, a movement of thousands of men and women who are giving their lives to impact the next generation of church and world leaders.

Keep your eyes open for the one-day seminars and trainings that organizations or local churches host. Those can be great cost-effective ways of getting training for not only yourself but also your volunteer team (but more on your team later).

You can also use books. Harry S. Truman once said, "Not all readers are leaders, but all leaders are readers." That's always stuck with me. I love to read, so it's easy for me. Others don't like to read as much, but reading still holds a lot of value. As I stated earlier, a lot of what I've learned in youth ministry has come from various authors. What's great about reading books is that new books are constantly coming out, offering new insights into ministry or new challenges in understanding theology. These are all good things. For the price of a college credit, you can build a helpful library to enhance your ministry training. I've listed some here that I think every youth leader should read.

- *The Youth Minister's Survival Guide* by Dr. Len Kageler. He was my college advisor and mentor. He's a wonderful guy, and it's a great book!
- *Your First Two Years in Youth Ministry* by Doug Fields

- *Youth Culture 101* by Walt Mueller. It's a great book on teen culture.
- *Apologetics for a New Generation* by Sean McDowell.
- *Sticky Faith* by Kara E. Powell and Chap Clark. This is an excellent resource!
- *Almost Christian* by Kenda Creasy Dean.
- *Soul Searching* by Melina Lundquist Denton and Christian Smith. It's a great book on connecting teens to faith.
- *Leading from the Second Chair* by Mike Bonem and Roger Patterson. This book contains excellent reminders on how we can serve our church from support roles.

These are just a few! There are so much more. Invest in books and reading materials! They not only help you learn for the role you want but can also help with your overall critical thinking.

In today's culture it's important for us to also use our online friends for input as well. While there are books being published and released on a regular basis, nothing is as fast as online resources. There are hundreds of sites and blogs out there that can help you get some great insight into the world of youth ministry. Check out the following sites:

- www.youthspecialties.com. It's a great site for resources and training events.
- www.downloadyouthministry.com. If you need some reproducible leader materials, last-minute game or easy prep messages, this is the site to go to! It's *by* youth pastors *for* youth pastors.

- www.simplyyouthministry.com. It's similar to the previous site but still very helpful!
- www.cpyu.org. This is a necessary site for *all* youth pastors/leaders. It's a great resource on culture stats, parenting tips, and ways we can connect parents and students together. It's a great site to point parents to as well!
- www.relevantmagazine.com. This one has some challenging articles. I don't always agree with them, but as my pastor says, "Chew the meat, spit out the bones."
- www.group.com. You should especially check out *Group Magazine*. At the time of this writing, they're offering it free online. It's an amazing resource for youth leaders. Everything inside is written by people in the trenches.

Here are some blogs I'd suggest to keep up with as well!

- www.morethandodgeball.com by Josh Griffin. Sign up for regular updates. Each one includes a fresh youth ministry article from an active youth pastor or leader.
- www.fulleryouthinstitute.org sponsored by Fuller Seminary. It's a must-read!
- www.jarrodjones.com. Jarrod is my current lead pastor, and he has a very real, very transparent blog on faith, health, and life.
- www.perrynoble.com. Perry is the lead pastor at NewSpring Church in South Carolina. I've always appreciated his down-to-earth view on ministry.
- http://kendadean.com. Kenda is a wonderful author and speaker!

All of these resources can be great assets!

Most of what I wrote in the previous section is primarily focused on a traditional education model. However, you may feel that's not the path you're on. Maybe you're a high school student who has sensed God's calling on your life to serve students? Maybe you have two vocations and you're not looking toward the more traditional path. Here's what I would suggest.

Internships

When I was in college, many of the internships that my friends and I held tended to be little more than glorified volunteer leader positions. We were given tasks to do, were allowed to teach from time to time, and were even allowed to plan events. It was helpful, but it could have been so much more. I would encourage you to spend some time in an internship with a local church to get some experience before you decide if youth ministry is the role you want to pursue.

If you're in high school and you're reading this, please pursue an internship now! Don't wait for college! If you're attending your church's student ministry, go speak to your pastor or director. Ask them for an internship opportunity now. Ask them to give you the behind-the-scenes look of ministry while you are deciding whether or not you want to pursue it. They can give you opportunities to lead ministries, try out some ideas, and somewhat see what it takes to do youth ministry. We started this a couple of years ago, and the results were incredible. Now I'll admit that our first HS student intern is not currently pursuing ministry as a full-time role. He thought about it early on, but he has since gone in a different professional direction. He did a great job, even though he had several moments of challenges. What his internship was able to do was show him what ministry entailed. It showed him enough to see that he didn't see himself as a full-time youth pastor. And that's okay! As he is going to school for a different career, he knows that he's had some experience and was able to make that decision with some support behind it. His choice wasn't based on theories. He is pursuing a career in occupational therapy, which he even sees has ministry potential. In addition, he is serving as a key volunteer in our student ministry at one of our campuses. He's a young man who can fill in to teach, lead a Bible study, and even lead a ministry event. I believe his intern time was very valuable for his faith and for his personal development. If you're not currently connected to your church's student ministry or if your church doesn't have one, please pray about reaching out to another local church for an internship opportunity.

If you're an adult coming from a different direction, maybe you're foregoing college because you've felt that school isn't something for you right now. Possibly you're making a career change. Maybe even you're retired and looking at this type of ministry as a new adventure. Regardless of where you're coming from, an internship would be awesome for you too! Consider connecting with the youth pastor at your church and asking him or her about this type of role. Give yourself a chance to see how things work on a day-to-day basis as you pray about pursuing a role in student ministry. It will give you a chance to see how you'd like the ministry before you make any decisions that could include major life changes.

Education comes in several different forms. I would encourage anyone going into student ministry to avoid the myth that it's based on fun and games and to realize that it's just as important as any other ministry in the church. Proverbs 22:6 (ESV) reminds us to "train up a child in the way he should go; even when he is old he will not depart from it." We get to a part of this training. If we're serious about this training, then we should go to great lengths to make sure we're being trained ourselves.

Chapter 3

Trying to Be Cool ... When We're Not

Cool. Hip. Relevant. Culturally connected. The words change, but the sentiment is still the same as it's been for years.

As student ministry leaders and workers, I'm sure we all want our students to like us, to think we're cool to hang with. But it's time for a reality check. Ready? Here it comes—

We're not cool!

At least not in the ways that many of us would like.

Over the years I've noticed that every part of our culture, regardless of the year or location, has certain demographics and assumptions. For example, when I talk to students about their lives and their futures, I hear many of them passionately describe their dreams and goals, and yet there seems to be a common thread among them. They're passionate about *not* becoming their parents! They claim, "I'm my own person. I'm an individual and unique!" They change their looks, hairstyles, personalities, and personal tastes. But when you look at an average group of teenagers, whether it's at a school or church, you notice one incredible thing. They all look the same! I don't say that as a judgment but as an interesting observation.

I've been blessed to be able to attend a number of training opportunities, including a nationwide convention for youth workers. One year the church I currently serve at allowed me to bring several of my team members with me. As we were leaving our hotel one morning, I was speaking to one of my leaders, and we were talking about this very thing. We did a small social experiment concerning youth leaders. At the time of the conversation, I was in my early thirties, and my leader was in his early twenties. We were from two different generations. I shared with him the following info: I observed that you could tell the age of the youth workers there by simply looking at the style of clothing they were wearing. I shared that anyone in my generation would probably be wearing jeans, sneakers, a backpack, and probably a sports hoodie/jersey. I also shared that his generation, the young to mid-twenties, would be wearing Birkenstock sandals and fleeces, and they would have beards and short, cropped haircuts. Also they would probably carry messenger bags with Nalgene bottles of water hanging from those bags too. We kept talking and laughing about it because we almost fit those descriptions. As we turned the corner and looked at the crowd, our jaws just about dropped. It was like the sheep and goats! The entire conference crowd had split and sectioned themselves to opposite sides of the road. One side contained my generation dressed as I thought, and the other side was filled with the millennials dressed as I had expected. It was a hilarious moment.

I attended the same conference two years ago and saw another generational change. Both of the previously mentioned groups were there, but the youngest millennials at the conference had a new look. It transitioned from the fleece and sandals to plaid and bushy hair and beards. Again, there's no judgment. This was just a curious observation.

What I've begun noticing from different groups is that when you walk in, it's hard to tell the difference between students and leaders, especially young leaders. When youth leaders are in their early twenties and possibly right out of college, it's understandable. But when youth workers in their late thirties or early forties, we really shouldn't worry about fitting in with them. I shutter when I meet a youth worker my age who has spent his recent days trading his Dockers for skinny jeans or her long skirt for a much shorter one, his favorite sports team jersey for a V-neck shirt and cardigan or her modest look for dark eyeliner and black nail polish—all in the name of "connecting" with students.

There's nothing wrong with opening ourselves up to the world our students live in—their music, their movies, and their social media. It helps us understand them, and we can use those items in small ways to reach students outside of our ministry circles. But if we're going to preach and teach our students about finding our identity in Christ, we certainly need to set the example and be ourselves inside and out!

Be yourself!

Galatians 2:20 (ESV) tells us, "I have been crucified with Christ. It is no longer I who live, but Christ who lives in me. And the life I now live in the flesh I live by faith in the Son of God, who loved me and gave himself for me."

Christ's sacrifice for us includes giving us an identity that isn't tied with anything in this world. We should be proud of the people He's made us to be. And we should be leading our students to the same conclusion. At the writing of this book, I'm a thirty-nine-year-old guy who could stand to lose a few pounds. I've had the same hairstyle since junior high, and I love wearing T-shirts and hoodies (especially those of my favorite Cleveland sports teams). Yes, I have no style, and I have a bland wardrobe. But it's comfortable for me. We have cable TV in our house with more than two hundred channels. We have dozens and dozens of DVDs, and we have a subscription to Netflix. But I find myself watching my favorite shows over and over, and most of them have been off the air for several years. But there is something relaxing to those, something secure and consistent. My students think I'm a bit boring in these areas. They like to make jokes about me, and we have a good laugh. But in the end it's those things that make me ... me. It's part of me as a pastor, husband, father, and friend. If I were to turn around, change my wardrobe and my lingo, and begin trying to be more like them, I would look like the guy who is trying to be their friend.

The danger is that we run the risk of trying to live on their level. While we want to be aware of their world and the culture they live in, we really should avoid trying to be identified by it. It's okay that we don't like the same things and see the world the same way. In fact, it's healthy that we don't.

Students need us to be the people God wants us to be. They need to see us being ourselves, pursuing our own passions, and living the lives we are called to live.

God has created you to be an incredible, creative, loving individual. We're doing Him a disservice by trying to be like someone else.

Setting the Example

One my absolute favorite verses in all of Scripture is 1 Timothy 4:12 (ESV), which says, "Let no one despise you for your youth, but set the believers an example in speech, in conduct, in love, in faith, in purity." I so wish I had known this verse while I was growing up. I spent so much time believing that people thought less of me because of my age. It used to completely frustrate and anger me. I would even act out in certain situations.

The first time I read this verse, I felt some worth. Even God was saying that I shouldn't let people use my age to treat me as a lesser person. It became one of the verses that fueled my passion for student ministry. Just because the students are in middle school and high school, that doesn't mean they can't change the world. In fact, I'm of the mind-set that teens do more to change the world than adults! Many adults are set in their ways, talking about change without actually acting on anything. Teens and twentysomethings are more active, more passionate, and at times more inclined to take a risk on something that they truly believe in. I've heard it said hundreds of times in hundreds of places, and I believe it completely. Students are not the church of tomorrow. They're the church of today. It's why the church *must* make student/youth ministry a priority. Without this demographic, I believe the church will die a slow death.

If we believe this about the generation of students that we're leading, the worst thing we can do is try to be like them and try to model ourselves after them. If we want them to truly be the church of today, then we need to set the example for them so that they can in turn set the example of others just as the book of Timothy says. How do we do this?

By being ourselves!

We can be ourselves in our speech. Ephesians 5:4 (ESV) clearly warns us, "Let there be no filthiness nor foolish talk nor crude joking, which are out of place, but instead let there be thanksgiving."

I love joking with students, laughing, even ribbing one another a bit. It builds camaraderie and relationships. However, there is a fine line with this. Even ribbing can quickly turn from friendly to insulting and demeaning. We have to make sure we keep that line clear. Our language needs to above reproach (1 Timothy 3). While quoting *The Office* may be a fun time with students, saying, "That's what she said," definitely crosses the line. Even if we're just repeating the quote, it's still inappropriate. We need to set the example for students by making sure we're controlling our tongues.

The tongue is so dangerous that James specifically gives us instructions on it. In James 3, he reminds us that while it's small, the tongue can create troubles beyond repair. And it's not just in the words we use. It's the attitude behind them.

Every teen culture tends to slightly distrust authority. That includes parents, governments, and yes, even us at times. The worst thing we can do is say anything to nurture those attitudes. We have to be very careful about what we portray to them. It's one thing to lend a listening ear to a young girl who's having major disagreements with her parents at home; it's another to communicate in any way that you agree with the girl and not her parents. If that moment happens, we've effectively contributed to the rift between them. I've been guilty of this on a couple of occasions early in ministry, and I have learned firsthand that sometimes the damage can be irreparable. And even if it's repaired between them, it can almost decidedly do damage to our credibility with parents. Students need us to support their parents' rules and guidelines. Yep, I said it! They *need* us to! Not because we will always agree with their parents, but they're going through enough turmoil personally and internally. They don't need the most influential adults in their lives creating more. If they see us unified with their parents/guardians, it will give them a sense of stability. They may not say that right away, and they may blame us for how hard life is for them; however, down the line they'll understand.

In conduct? How can we set the example in conduct? We simply shouldn't do anything that violates the Bible. I've had people in my past challenge me to ask myself, "If Jesus was sitting there with you, would you do that?" Either way, Scripture lays out for us the expectations of our behavior. We should set the bar high for our students on how we spend our time. Obviously our students should never see us walking out of bars drunk, going into adult theaters, or going out on romantic dates with people who aren't our spouses. Those are the obvious ones! What about the gray areas? My leaders are forbidden to attend a R-rated movies with students regardless of the content. But I can't forbid them from watching these in their free time. But I do challenge them to think about the message they send to students who see them going into those movies. I don't think every youth worker in the world will ever agree on a set list of rules, and we shouldn't. We're all different. But I always challenge them to just think. If they decide to do it, then they'll be able to answer any questions.

We should also set the example in our conduct with students of the opposite sex, especially for those youth workers who take positions right out of college. I'm not questioning anyone's character, but this is an area *every* youth worker can be attacked in. It's natural for students, especially students who have unsettled home lives, to develop strong attachments to adults they trust. And it's common for us as youth workers to connect with some students more than others. We just need to be very careful on how we build those connections. We need to make sure that we're building proper boundaries and that our actions are worthy to Christ. Keep in mind that others students are watching. If our conduct is questionable in any way, it will affect our relationships with the other students. It can be damaging to our reputations and ultimately the character of Christ.

Setting the example in love, faith, and purity should follow the same path as those previously mentioned. In the end, what ultimately matters is our character. It's why it's so important for us to be ourselves. As we follow Jesus, we lead others to Him. If we're spending too much time recreating ourselves so that we fit in with our students, then we're missing the opportunity to lead them to where we want them to go.

Be yourself!

Chapter 4

Questions, Questions, Questions

If you're reading this and you're a parent, you'll understand.

I've come to enjoy the word *why*.

Not because it's a great piece of English culture. Not because it gives us a massive amount of information. But because I was pummeled into submission with it.

When I became a dad, I loved just staring at my daughter. I would just stare at her as she grew and began doing some cool things. Then I couldn't wait till she started talking. My wife and I loved hearing her jabber, coo, and try to imitate the words we were saying. Then came *mommy* and *daddy*, and we were excited. Then came the day she said the word *why*.

If you're a parent, you know what this is like. Now every conversation includes hundreds of *why* questions from the child. I have to admit, it got annoying. Sometimes I'd like to say, "It's nap time," without endless explanations. Or I'd want to say, "Let's put your toys away," without having to discuss the philosophies of such an action. But as time went on, God blessed us with more kids. And each one followed the same path. As the kids grew, I began to really enjoy them asking why. Crazy, right? But I began to understand that they were just trying to learn, trying to figure out what is going on around them, learning the boundaries, finding their way. Asking why was their way of communicating with us. Don't get me wrong. My son definitely used it as a bargaining tool to get ten more minutes of TV or avoid putting things away. But all in all, questions are incredibly valuable.

One thing that I didn't take advantage of early in my ministry career was asking questions. I fell into the trap of thinking that because I had both a bachelor's and a master's degree, I knew better than everyone who had been there. I didn't take into consideration that as many degrees as I had, I didn't have experience or history at that church to make great decisions. I wish I had taken the time to ask questions.

Questions aren't a sign of weakness. I've learned that they're a sign of wisdom and humility.

When we arrive at a ministry, it's good to remember that the ministry didn't suddenly appear when we arrived. The church/ministry has a history. It has had multiple staff members and congregation members who may have been there for many years. In fact, depending on your age, you may meet congregation members who have been there longer than you've been alive! There is a wealth of information out there just inside your ministry building, all of which will benefit us in our long-term ministry careers.

Ask your lead/senior pastor.

This is your biggest ally in your ministry regardless of your ministry's reporting structure or where you fall on the totem pole of leadership. Your lead/senior pastor can "make you or break you." Obviously it's not that dramatic. But the sentiment is there. If your lead/senior pastor supports you, it can take a tremendous amount of pressure off of you. During my time of serving in student ministry, I've had the privilege of serving for various lead/senior pastors. Each relationship has been unique. They've all had their ups and downs. I've learned a lot from each of them. But it wasn't until I arrived at our current ministry that I took the time to ask questions and learn. When I did that, I began to learn more and more. I learned not just about the history of the church I was serving at or the pastor's opinions on issues but also more and more about how wise he was in ministry. In his fifty years of ministry, he has pretty much seen it all. There wasn't a situation I could bring up that he hadn't experienced. He was able to mentor me in several ways, ways that I hadn't encountered before. In fact, he even put together a binder of ministry articles that covered multiple ministry situations. We would work through them weekly, and I was able to gain so much wisdom from him.

However, we gain the most wisdom when we ask questions. No question should be glossed over and go unasked. We can't learn if we don't ask. Taking the time to ask questions is invaluable!

Ask questions of other church leaders too!

- Talk to elders. These people are generally the spiritual *checks and balances* of the church. They have probably been around for several years and can answer just about any question you have. They can share the spiritual history of the church. I love talking to some of our elders, especially the ones who have been at our church since its beginning. They have amazing stories and incredible wisdom!

- Talk to existing staff. Find out the stories from past staff members by asking about what they've seen transpire over the years. They can also share with you some of the skeletons from the past. I'm not talking about gossiping about the past. I'm talking about things that have happened behind closed doors that can serve as teachable moments for you as you move forward.
- Talk to deacons and deaconesses. These people compose the team that should have the most interaction with the congregation members. In our current church, these folks handle meals and visitations. Some host outreaches and even serve Communion. They have a great amount of information to share with you! This information can help you learn the culture of the church.

Ask questions of former staff members.

I think this technique is completely appropriate; however, you should choose who you speak to wisely. For example, I believe you should always speak to your predecessor. I know it can be awkward, but who can give you the best information on the role you're considering other than the one who just left it? They can share a lot of fresh insights and a lot of fresh stories. Even if they left under contentious circumstances, it's still a good call to make. Chat with them. Ask them about the good and the bad of their experience. It's not about finding dirt on what happened, and it's not about giving them an audience to vent. However, they are the best ones to tell you about the reality of the role. It doesn't mean that they're 100 percent right or 100 percent wrong. What it does mean is that they're human, and for whatever reason, they moved on to a new experience.

Here is my disclaimer on this point because it can be a bit touchy. If you know that your predecessor was dismissed for any kind of moral or ethical reason, I would reconsider reaching out to him or her. Chances are that this person agreed to step away to keep the entire church from finding out about what happened. If this is the case, reaching out to this person could rip open a wound and cause more damage than good.

Tap into the church veterans.

Most churches have that man or that woman. You know which one I'm talking about. I'm referring to the older gentleman who knows everyone and everything about the church. He seems to have served on every committee in the church at some point. She's the older woman who seems to know every family as if she was the church's grandmother. When someone is sick, she seems to be the one who makes soup or bakes something. They're at every church service and every business meeting, and they seem to be in the building every time it's open. They carry around a tattered Bible with bulletins from a decade ago. Their Bibles are marked up with notes of wisdom from years of study. They have notes from pastors who haven't served there in years. They have stories for every situation you can imagine. These are the people to bombard with questions. You should absorb all that they can share with you.

Ask a mentor.

Every pastor should have a mentor. Mentors can be church veterans or other church leaders who are a bit more experienced. They can even be people outside of your church too. You can ask these people about anything and expect an honest and unbiased answer. I'm not saying that you won't get honest answers from people inside your church. However, I think we all know that there are questions that we can ask that some people won't be able to answer, some questions that may be too sensitive for current congregation members or leaders to speak on. These mentors give you a chance to ask those questions and get answers that you can learn from.

Questions are amazing learning tools for us. Too many people think they know it all and don't need to ask questions. In ministry, it's one of the easiest ways for us to learn.

Chapter 5

Big Church v. Small Church

This is one of touchiest subjects in church circles. The major assumption is that big churches are cold and uncaring and that small churches are dead. Unfortunately it's church people making those statements.

Those from a smaller church (a hundred people or less) look at larger churches as sheep-stealing, uncaring places only about making money and putting on a great show. I've heard this several times over the years. I'm sure it comes from a little bit of fear, possibly a slight bit of jealousy, and maybe even a little bit of hurt over those who have left to attend those larger churches. On the other side, there are many larger churches that see some smaller churches as old-school, dead churches who are only hanging on because the key families won't let them go. This may come from a little bit of arrogance, a bit of elitism, and possibly a bit of hurt for those who attended a smaller church in the past and didn't feel like they were really discipled and cared for.

The honest truth is that both sides are *wrong!* They're wrong in their assumptions. They may be right in some situations across the world. Anyone in church ministry knows that there are large churches more driven by the spotlight and that there are some smaller churches that exist because they just enjoy hanging together and won't let their church go. But neither is 100 percent true across the board. And if we make those assumptions across the board, the only thing we accomplish is damaging the image of the bride of Christ.

As student pastors/directors/leaders, the allure of a large church can be overwhelming. Maybe you've been through this, maybe not. But think of this situation: A young man graduating from college with a youth ministry degree and a desire for a position in student ministry receives two calls. Call one comes from a small local church. The church is smaller in attendance (about 150 to 160 on a Sunday). It has about eight to nine students in the ministry. Salary isn't much, but it's enough to get by on. The church is predominantly older families, and much of the leadership is related. He hears the phrase "We want to reach the youth. They're the future of the church," but You wonder what they mean by that since there aren't a lot of young families in the church. The pastor is a good guy and a good preacher, and he loves the Lord.

The second call comes in from a much larger church. There are multiple staff members and multiple large ministries. The salary is much larger, and the budget is much larger. The ministry has ten times the amount of students the small church has. It has a tremendous reputation in the community, and it looks like a dream job. The church is predominantly young adults and young families. The church's look, feel, and sound are very culturally relevant. It's a place he might attend even if he weren't looking for a job there.

For many of us, church number two sounds like the Disney World of jobs. We can start visualizing all of the options we would have with more students, a bigger budget, and more space. We look at the larger ministry space and think of all of the cool toys we could put in there, all of the ministry options we can pursue. We start dreaming of all of the things we've been trained to do. And for some of us—if we're honest with ourselves—we actually feel a sense of pride that a church like this called us to potentially join their team. It's as if we put that church on a pedestal.

We might sour ourselves on the smaller church. The flash isn't there. We may find ourselves in a comparison battle, using each church to measure the others. In the business world, marketing world, even in the world of professional sports, this method works perfectly! If you're working your way up the ladder in the business world, you wouldn't take a job at a smaller firm if a larger one is offering you the same job! If you're a professional athlete, you're not taking less money to go to a team that isn't a winning team in your opinion. No football player takes less money to play for the Oakland Raiders when the New England Patriots are pursuing him. It just doesn't happen.

But in ministry we can never use that formula to choose a church. If you do, you're cheating the church out what might be best for them. You're damaging your ministry by choosing in the flesh, and you're insulting Jesus Christ because you're not willing to trust Him by choosing the place you believe He wants you to be! We don't have crystal balls, so we can't guess about what is going to happen in the future. If we trust in Christ and His calling on our lives, we need to make sure we choose our opportunity with great care and faith.

Maybe you're in this situation now. Maybe you're reading this book while you're deciding between these two situations. My intention for writing this book is to help other student and youth ministers find their way in ministry and find the path that will help them stay in it for the long haul. If we're not committed in the long term, students will know and will base their trust off of that. Whether it's eight students or eight hundred, they need their pastor/director/leader to follow the path that God lays out, not the one in the shinier package. As someone who has had the privilege of serving in both, let me share with you some pros and cons of each.

Serving at a Smaller Church

Here's a pro: Everyone knows you! There is something definitely comforting about serving in a setting where everyone in the church knows you. It helps you (and your family) feel a sense of church family. It's great when your kids are sick or a tragedy strikes, and the entire church surrounds you with prayer and support. It also helps you build a solid sense of accountability. With a smaller staff, it's easier to share and discuss things with those you serve under. And it allows them to dig deeper into your life, ask you the tough questions, and push you to grow spiritually. It will help you build your credibility as well. In the smaller setting, people not only hear about what you're doing, but they can see you in action as well. Parents of young kids can see the ministry you're building, and it can excite them for the future. Smaller churches can be an amazing blessing!

Now here's a con too: Everyone knows you! While it can be a blessing, it can also be a little overwhelming. You can feel like you're under a microscope all of the time. You can feel that while your victories are well seen, so are your mistakes. You can feel like you have no room to grow and stretch. Conflicts can spread easier because of the smaller amount of people. Simple conflicts between two people can be blown out of proportion easier. Because people feel like they know you, it can make you feel like it takes more effort to rebound from tough decisions or mistakes. Serving at a smaller church does have its challenges, but they're nothing that can't be overcome.

Smaller groups are easier to build into! When you're the leader of small youth group, it gives you a huge leg up on getting to know everyone. And you can know them on a deeper level. It gives you some amazing opportunities to really help each student so that they allow God prune them and weed out the negative. You can address each student one-on-one about their spiritual growth. When you walk into the room during your group meeting, you can address each student. You can really lay a good foundation for the ministry by allowing each person to have a say in the direction and goals of the ministry. It can be an incredibly tight, close-knit ministry.

However, smaller groups can tend to hit their ceiling very early. In my opinion, smaller groups can hit their ceiling quicker than larger groups. This is not because the ministry is any easier or because the students are any more holy, but if you're at a smaller church, you may not have the same amount of new kids each year. It can be easy for the kids in a smaller group to feel like they've reached their max quicker because they know you and know everyone in the group. It can take a large amount of creativity to keep things fresh and create the path for students to follow.

Smaller groups have a unique culture too. The culture of your group will be very organic and personal, and it can be molded after the students who attend. When you take your group to serve in the community, it can be a little more impactful on your ministry. A smaller group can allow these events to build teams even more. The culture becomes much more student-based than leader-based. There are a lot of things that smaller groups can do. Spontaneous events are easier to pull off because only a small number of parents need to be contacted. Spontaneous events are easier because arrangements are just for a small number of people. When a group is smaller, positivity and energy can spread and ignite the group in amazing ways! Smaller groups just have a different feel, a different atmosphere. And that's a good thing!

However, just as positivity and energy can spread quickly in a smaller group, the same goes for negativity. When you're ministering to a small group and attitudes turn negative, it can act as a poison too. I have nothing against leadership, but it's the nature of group dynamics. If it gets too bad, it can feel like the inmates are running the asylum. It can be overwhelming. It also can be a little bit of challenge. When you're planning any type of event (whether fun- or service-focused), each student who cannot come puts a huge dent into your number of participants. Like with most groups of teenagers, when one doesn't want to go, it can trickle down, especially if it's a close-knit group. If one friend doesn't want to go, the others may not want to as well.

Serving at a larger church:

Here you can be as known as whatever you want to be. I don't like the spotlight. I hate people singing to me at birthdays. I don't do well with compliments, and I don't want to have the spotlight. If you're like me, serving at a larger church may be helpful. I know that sounds weird, but there is an incredible amount of freedom when you're not worried about the spotlight. It's why I try to lead by example and instill in my students the fact you shouldn't crave a thank-you when you serve and honor God. The freedom can allow you to take some chances and make some mistakes, and you won't feel like everyone will make you pay for it forever. This isn't a bad thing because it gives you freedom to establish the ministry's reputation slowly and deliberately.

On the other hand, the same freedom can work against you. It's one thing to be out of the spotlight, but it's another to be a phantom. Out of the spotlight means you don't want attention. Being a phantom means you don't want accountability or connection. We can't have that. We have to make sure that we are involved enough that people in the church see us as assets, as ministers and not just babysitters for older kids or games coordinator for teens. If we end up with the latter of those descriptions, we need to ask ourselves how involved we are. We don't have to do things to gain attention. We don't have to be the wild, outlandish personalities that do things to gain attention. But we can do things that people take notice of in positive ways. For example, do you serve anywhere else in your church? We can kid ourselves into thinking that we're so busy we can't do anything other than student ministry. Are we helping in the children's ministry? Are we helping the parking team when they're shorthanded? Are we tossing salt on the icy parking lot after a storm? Are we greeting people at the door when we have a service off? Doing those things helps let the church, your pastor, your staff, and your students see that you have a servant's heart. And more importantly, you set the tone for your ministry and your leaders.

Larger groups allow for a greater influence radius too. While smaller groups allow for deeper relationships, leading a larger ministry allows you to have a wider influence radius. You connect in some form with a greater number of students at each ministry event. It can widen your ministry influence. When you speak at an event with eight to ten students, you can make it more pointed. When you speak to fifty or sixty people, you have the opportunity to share the gospel with more students. The hope is that those students will share that message with fifty or sixty more, and the ripple effect goes on and on. With the larger ministry comes a larger team of leaders to serve alongside. As you build into each leader, they can turn and influence others. In my situation at my current ministry, most of my student ministry leaders serve in other ministries. As I have a chance to invest into them, I am confident that they then turn around and invest in others in the other places they serve. That's the ripple effect.

However, larger groups require more intentional influence. When we are serving in a large ministry, we have to make sure that we are being very intentional about our investing and influences. In my opinion, we cannot take the "water balloon" approach to influence. Ever throw a water balloon? What happens? It hits the ground, explodes, and whoever is near the explosion gets wet. Sometimes in larger groups, leaders find themselves doing their jobs, and those near the leaders benefit from the experience. A leader's influence is extended more because of proximity to others, not because of a plan or intentionality. If we lead larger ministries, we need to spend more time targeting and planning about who we influence and how we influence them. It takes more time, but the rewards are immeasurable!

Larger ministries can allow for a long term, more intentional discipleship plan. As I mentioned previously, I believe that sometimes smaller groups reach their maximum ceiling in terms of growth (both in number and in spiritual maturity), but not because you as the leader have done anything wrong or because you haven't been pursuing Jesus on your own. I believe it mainly happens because smaller groups generally don't have a large influx of new faces on a regular basis. As the leader of a larger ministry, you're more likely to gain a group of new faces every fall. Again, this is not because you as the leader are a teen magnet, but if you're part of a larger church, then the chances are you're going to see more new faces in your church. More new faces in your church means a better chance for more new faces in your ministry. This will help create a long-term opportunity for ongoing discipleship. This should keep the ministry from reaching its ceiling for a very long time.

However, larger ministries have to create more discipleship options. The larger your ministry is, the more personalities you have to attend to. That means a cookie-cutter approach to discipleship cannot be as effective. It's not because the model isn't effective but because each person is different and everyone learns differently. More people means we have to look for more ways to disciple students. That strategy can include small groups, one-on-one meetings, Bible studies, etc. To offer only one can limit the ministry's impact. The more we offer, the greater impact we can have! We also have to be willing to recreate our methods as time goes because as culture changes, so must our methods.

Our current pastor loves to challenge us by reminding us that if our ministry doesn't look different three years from now, then we're probably not challenging ourselves enough. And at times that can be true. But I think it's important for us to keep asking, "Are our methods still working?" If we don't, we can unintentionally create sacred cows. And those start to become objects of worship. However, because we need to create more options, it requires more time, energy, resources, and most of all, people

But serving at a larger church will give you many more potential leaders! Think about it! At a smaller church, you're probably competing with other ministries for leaders, or there just aren't too many leaders who want to invest in teenagers. This can be especially true if the demographic of your church is older in age. Many people don't mind holding babies in your children's ministry. They may not even mind sitting with the two- and three-year-olds and teaching them. But to invest in teenagers takes a lot more, and it takes certain people to want to do it. We also have to face reality. When you serve in some ministries, it's a weekend commitment, and once Sunday is over, they're off till next weekend. That's not a criticism, but it's the nature of certain ministries. If you're serving at a larger church, the belief is that there are plenty of people to serve in every ministry! So when you're looking for adult leaders, you have a much bigger pool to choose from. And since the pool is bigger, there is a better chance you'll be able to find the right members for your team.

However, serving at a larger church means you *need* to find more leaders! When you have a smaller group, say eight to ten students, two leaders can usually handle any event or ministry. When you have a larger group, in order to keep things safe, you need more people. If you want to add different discipleship options, you need people to implement those and lead those. While you are in a small group, you have a little less pressure to find people right away. If it's small, then you can play the waiting game when it comes to finding leaders. When you're leading a larger ministry, the waiting can't be as long. It requires us, the main leaders, to be aggressive in finding, recruiting, and training leaders on a regular basis. We need to be consistently looking for and praying for new leaders to come and help continue to build the ministry. It needs to be in the top three entries on our priority list. It takes time and energy, and we have to hold ourselves to a standard of excellence, not always in results but in expectations and character.

The reality is that the size of the church doesn't matter. I plead with you not to let the size of the church impact your decision. There is something very flattering about a larger church pursuing you and wanting you to join their team. It can almost become a pride issue. We can find ourselves looking at the size of a church or ministry as a badge of honor and a sign of our skills instead of God's blessing and higher responsibility.

On the flip side, we can overlook smaller churches because we convince ourselves that "it will never work." Or as I stated previously, we've convinced ourselves that smaller churches are always less healthy or dying. Both assumptions are absolutely dangerous.

When you are choosing a church, especially your first church, keep these things in mind:

1) Above anything else, ask yourself, "Is God leading me there?" There have been some that have chosen a

ministry spot based on other options—size, salary, group demographic, proximity to family/friends, etc. None of those things are necessarily bad. But they should be secondary to the place that God has called you to. If God hasn't called you there, then it's not worth trying. We won't succeed, and we won't be honoring the Lord.

2) Does it fit *you*? We are all wired differently, so make sure the church fits you. Don't be so blind that you don't see your weaknesses or the areas where you can improve. But also don't settle for a place where you can't see yourself fitting in. Think of things like music style, preaching style, dress code, ministry focus, etc. These are things you should think about before you accept a role, not because they're overly important but because these things need to fit you and how you're wired. If they don't fit you completely, are they things that you can work with? For example, if you do not enjoy worshipping to hymns, then you may want to think twice about serving at a church that relies heavily on them. If you do serve there, you do so knowing that you'll have to adjust to the music style. I don't believe music style is everything; however, we need to be able to worship freely and for our own growth. Again, I'm not saying you should refuse a church whose worship style isn't your favorite. I'm saying you should at least think through it.

3) Will they invest in you there spiritually, emotionally, and professionally? This is one area I wish I had taken more seriously when I was choosing my first full-time ministry. I'm not saying that my first full-time church didn't try to take care of me. I'm saying I wish I had asked more questions

about these areas before I had gone so that I could have been more prepared. I went into that role with expectations that weren't shared by others. Make sure that the preaching is preaching that you can learn and grow from. If you find yourself becoming bored or feeling like you are not connecting with it, then maybe it's not the right place for you. As ministers, you will spend a great amount of time giving of yourself. You need to make sure you're being fed and nourished. It's vital to our own spiritual growth. How about emotionally? Will you be surrounded by others who will love you and lift you up with life gets rough? Will you have accountability so that your own emotions don't end up doing damage to you or others? Will the church you're looking to serve at help you grow professionally? Will books, blogs, websites, seminars, conferences, and other resources be available to you? Will they provide resources to help you grow as a minister, leader, and follower of Jesus? All of these are important if you are truly going to be able to minister to students as Jesus leads you! If these aren't available, then think hard about whether or not this is the place for you.

4) Does the church *value* student ministry. This is extraordinarily important! Please make sure the church truly values student ministry. We provide resources to what we value! The good news is that they're interviewing you for a role as a minister to teenagers. So that's a good start! As you visit and interview, look around. Are students pieces of the church community, or are they seen more as background noise (for lack of a better term) and a labor

force? Do they have a designated space, or are they in shared space? A shared space isn't bad if it's necessary because of building capacity or room availability. Sometimes we have to adjust to fit into the overall ministry picture of the church. However, there are times when students are in a shared space because space focused on students isn't seen as a need. A room is just a room, but to students it's their place to be themselves. Is student ministry prayed over regularly? Is it a regular line item on budget and board meetings? Does the church see students as disciples? Or is the church just waiting for them to grow up and become adults when they can "really be useful to the church"? All of these are signs of how a church sees their teenagers. If teenagers don't feel valued at a church, they won't attend. They need to feel valued for who they are, not for who people want them to be. If a church values them for who they are, they will give their time, talents, and treasures to that church community. If the church you are interviewing with doesn't seem to value teenagers, then you should think long and hard about whether or not this is the place for you. It's not because they're not good people who love Jesus but because you may find yourself very frustrated early on.

Chapter 6

Leadership 101

> Leadership is not about titles, positions or flowcharts. It is about one life influencing another.
> —John C. Maxwell

John Maxwell is one of the country's top authorities on leadership. He's a celebrated speaker, author, and consultant. His books line the shelves in my office, and I routinely give them out to others. I love what he has to say, his wisdom, and his communication style. He is a highly recommended read for those in any type of leadership role.

I say this because if you're a youth pastor/director, you're a leader!

In our current day and age, leadership is such a misunderstood and overused concept. Granted, leadership comes in different forms.

- Leadership can come from people's jobs or role titles. Maybe they're in charge. Maybe they're bosses. Yes, staff must obey what these people say to do. That doesn't

mean that they are leading. That just means they are accomplishing a task.
- Leadership also comes in the form of some sort of ranking. I always think of the military ranking. There are titles that rank above other titles. Those of the lower rank would not dare to disturb or upset those of a higher ranking because that kind of action carries stiff punishment. Those leaders are obeyed and followed because their title and ranking warrants it.
- Leadership also comes in the form of the person that everyone seems to follow because he or she seems to garner the most attention. This isn't always a positive thing. For instance, consider the class clown who is always the center of attention in school. Pretty soon he'll have others repeating his same shtick in other classes, trying to get the same recognition and laughs. Now this class clown isn't a traditional leader, but he does find himself leading people, albeit in the wrong direction. But you also have good students who try to live right and follow Jesus, and people genuinely like them. When they move toward something, people will tend to follow. They don't have the title, but they are certainly leaders.

Before I go any further, please don't think that I'm saying the people previously mentioned don't have leadership skills. For example, the higher-ranking military leader may ooze leadership skills. And others may follow them because of their characters and ethics and not solely because of the title and ranking. But even if that is true, their ranking becomes the most obvious. Team captains, CEOs, directors, prime ministers, presidents, and grand poobahs all have amazing opportunities to impact lives! They can do this once they realize that people want to be led and inspired, not pushed and bossed around.

Leadership is something that we as youth pastors and leaders need to be very diligent about pursuing. It's something that students are desperately looking for. They're not looking for people with the best ideas, the coolest clothes, the soul patch on the chin, or someone who they can pal around with. They want adults who will guide and lead them to where God wants them to be. We need to be those types of leaders.

Dos and Don'ts of Student Ministry Leaders

Consider these things all student ministry leaders must do (or at least be willing to do).

Be a servant leader. There is one quote that I heard years ago that has always stuck with me. I cannot remember who said it, but I've heard it several times through seminary and ministry. It says that "a leader cannot lead people where they haven't been themselves." We cannot take students to any level of faith if we haven't been there ourselves. That doesn't mean we must have experience with everything by a young age. But as pastors/leaders/directors, it would be incredibly difficult for us to try to lead another person to a place where we haven't been but not because it's not a good place; however, if we haven't been there, how do we know if we've arrived there? For example, a person who has never had any experience in football could not suddenly coach an NFL team to a Super Bowl. If the person hasn't been exposed to the subject before, he or she just doesn't have the inside knowledge about what it takes to get there.

If we want our students to be the type of disciples that want to live like Jesus, we have to be servant leaders. We have to be the example through our lifestyles, our attitudes, and our desires. In my experience what this means is that we need to be the first to arrive and the last to leave. We should be the ones who step up to help meet needs not just in our ministry but in the church and in the community as well. When our students see us doing these things, it shows them that ministry isn't about a job. It's about serving others. Just as the Maxwell quote from the beginning of this chapter says, leadership is "one life influencing another."

At our church it's not uncommon for my students to see me mopping floors, painting offices, taking out the trash, etc. And it's not because I want a thank-you or attention, but I want my students and my kids to see how important serving is regardless of the role.

Leaders are learners. I learn the truth of this statement more and more as each year passes. I've always been someone who likes to learn. I'm the type of person who gets fascinated with how things work. I find myself watching documentaries on leadership structures, on how they are created, on why each role is what it is, and on how it all fits together. I enjoy watching home improvement shows on home flips and seeing how they make things come together. I love shows on inventions so that I can geek out when I see how they tinker with each item and put it together. I know I'm a dork. But it's helped me change my thinking. As I head into each situation of ministry, I find myself analyzing and rethinking every angle just to find the best path. I know most leaders probably do the same thing. And I also know that there are many leaders who are sharper than me and can go through that process quicker. I've begun to see the importance of constant learning. As youth leaders/pastors/directors, we should always look for ways to better ourselves in our ministry roles. We should be constantly learning about Scripture, about teens, about culture, about psychology, etc. We have a lot of options besides books, including podcasts, blogs, websites, etc. We should take advantage of every option available to us. If we're not learning, we're not growing. If we're not growing, we're not leading. That's when our leadership becomes stale and stagnant. When that happens, our ministry begins to wither and die.

Find a mentor. None of us has all of the answers. No matter how smart we are, how many degrees we have, or how many books we read, we still need help. We still need guidance. There is no greater resource we can find than a mentor. I've been blessed over the years to have several men who have spoken into my life. Rudy Sheptock was my first youth pastor. While I was only in youth group for one year—I came to believe in Christ at the beginning of my senior year of high school—he had a huge impact on me. He was one of the examples I had in my mind when I followed God's call into student ministry. He was fun and goofy (in a good way), and he had a tremendous love for Jesus. What was most impactful for me was the way he accepted me as the person I was, and he invested in me too. I can't thank him enough. I also want to mention John Kitchen, who mentored me during my ordination period. He was extraordinarily encouraging, and he was a blast to hang out with. He has a great love of Jesus and for his church. I admire him as a man as much as a pastor. The most impactful thing John did for me was push me when I thought I didn't want to be pushed. During my ordination process, my wife and I had our second child (a baby girl), who developed some complications shortly after birth. It was a difficult time for me to focus while my daughter was hospitalized. I went to him and said that I wanted to postpone my ordination process for a year so that I could refocus. But John wouldn't let me. He lovingly challenged me. He said that I was ready and that I wouldn't necessarily be more ready if we waited. I followed his guidance and completed the process with God's grace and strength. I will always be grateful to him for pushing me. Both of these men plus a number of others have helped me become the husband, father, pastor, and follower of Jesus that I am today.

Books can teach a lot. However, there is something about having people in your life who just don't teach you facts. They listen to you, reprimand you when you're out of line, celebrate with you when you see victories, and pick you up when things go wrong. Most of all, no matter what is going on in your life or ministry, they constantly point you back to the person of Jesus, the ultimate mentor.

Mentor someone else. The apostle Paul built into and ministered with Timothy. Timothy had Titus, and he took what he had learned from Paul and invested in Titus. It's a great example of the mentoring relationship we should all try to emulate. It's a great example of discipleship in its truest sense. Just as I encourage all of you to find mentors, I think it's just as important for us to mentor another. Thankfully, as we serve in student ministry, there is no shortage of mentoring opportunity. We should be taking a student or two under our wing and investing in them. We shouldn't focus just on church stuff either. Get them involved with your family. Let them see you with your spouse and kids. Let them see how you treat the one you're dating. Let them be involved in your personal life in appropriate ways. Share your experiences, your stories, your mistakes, and your victories. By doing so, you're taking what God has taught you and passing it on to the next generation.

Be a team player. As much as we want it to be, student ministry isn't why the church exists. I say that with a tongue-in-cheek tone, but I think I can speak for many of my colleagues when I say that student ministry can at times feel like it's seen as the least important ministry in the church. While I can't speak for every church, I think the majority would say that is a wrong assumption. Personally, I believe that it can seem like the forgotten ministry because unless you're called to serve in it, it can seem like such a foreign entity that is hard to understand. Many people don't get teens, don't understand them, and therefore aren't really motivated to be around them. I bring this up because it's so easy to turn the wagons inward and just focus on us when we think we're the forgotten group. The greatest travesties in student ministry are the pastors who keep their students out of the life of the overall church. I'm not saying youth-only activities or services are bad, but they can't be all that's offered. (I will address this subject later.)

As a youth pastor/leader/director, make sure that you're part of the bigger picture and the church's bigger plan. If you are only involved with students, you're doing yourself a huge disservice. And more importantly, you're cheating your church out of what you can offer. Jump in and help! Serve in the children's ministry. Lead the adult Bible study once in a while. Ask to preach on Sunday or during a special service. Offer to help the maintenance team with spring cleaning. Help in any way you can to be a part of the bigger plan. In my current ministry situation, I routinely preach at our communion services, pray at other church events, lead classes, offer baby dedications, serve in the nursery, teach kindergarten, paint rooms, and help mop floors after spills. It's helped me build credibility with the congregation, but it also solidifies my heart so that I feel like part of the team.

And these are things all student ministry leaders must not do at all costs!

Do *not* be your students' buddy. Yes, we need to have friendly relationships with them, even family-type relationships. But we cannot treat them like friends. If we do, we forfeit the ability to speak the harder truths into their lives. They don't need us to be their friends, they need us to be mentoring leaders for them. They need us to be people they can trust, but they need to know that we will say and do what we think is best for them, even if it means upsetting them.

Now this doesn't mean that every time you're with your students, you need to have a sit-down formal Bible study. We need to have social time with them by going to ball games and movies, playing sports and video games, eating pizza or wings, going swimming, etc. We can do all of those things with them. However, I would really encourage you to keep the mind-set that you're their leader, not just one of the group. I've seen where youth leaders blurred that line, and it has led to questionable decisions and inappropriate actions and relationships.

Keep watch on your social media. Social media can be a great tool. I personally use Facebook to keep up with friends and family, but it's also great to make announcements for ministry events. Twitter is helpful as well, although it's a bit more limited because of the 140-character cap. Instagram is a great tool to promote ministry events, and you can show others what's happening in the ministry. However, all of these and others can be incredibly damaging as well. Be super careful with what you put out there. I've learned the hard way that things you may mean in good fun or things with no intended meaning at all can blow up in your face! Sometimes we can even find ourselves airing our dirty laundry on social media as a passive-aggressive way of making sure someone out there knows what we're are thinking and feeling. We're humans. We can sometimes lose control of our emotions. But as James 3:1–12 reminds us, as leaders we need to control our tongues. While that includes speech, it also includes what we type and post. We cannot fall victim to that temptation. It solves nothing and only causes more issues.

The same goes for any articles/posts that you decide to repost. Sometimes you can just post funny memes or jokes that are out there, and people will give a laugh and possibly repost. But sometimes those funny things aren't funny to everyone. I remember about a year ago I reposted a meme about the idea that cats are evil. I can't remember the exact wording, but the picture was just too funny. I can't stand cats, so I posted it just for a laugh. The next day I received a Facebook message, a *long* one about how I had offended a church member who loved her cats. She had multiple cats, and they were like her kids. Essentially I was calling her kids evil. She even threatened to call our pastor and elders to have me disciplined. I laughed for about an hour—not at the picture but at how ridiculous her reaction was. However, when I stepped back and prayed, I realized that whether I agreed with her or not, whether I understand or not, I offended her. I quickly called her, spoke to her, and apologized to her, and she was gracious because she knew that I had posted it for fun. Even as I type this, I think it was a crazy reaction, but in the end, as leaders, we have to avoid that type of *trouble*. I still post things I think are funny, but I try to think through them a bit more. You will meet people who, no matter what you post, will find it upsetting. We can't please everyone all of the time. But I think we can certainly filter things better.

When it comes to social media, I'd also encourage you to be selective on what social media you engage in. I use Twitter, Facebook, and Instagram. (I use them at the time of this writing, but who knows what else will be out there by the time you're reading this?) As I have said, I think they are okay if we're willing to use them wisely. However, I caution my leaders against others. Personally I would not encourage any youth leader to use mediums like Snapchat. It's not that it's a bad site. But what you send disappears after a few seconds. Even when you look at the app's rating info, it says, "Rated 12+ for the following: Infrequent/mild profanity or crude humor, infrequent/mild/mature/suggestive themes, infrequent/mild alcohol, tobacco, or drug use or references, infrequent/mild sexual content and nudity." As leaders, we should always be beyond reproach (1 Timothy 4:12), and sites like this can compromise that simply because things can be sent and/or seen and then disappear without a trace. It can open us up to suspicion and worry that we don't need to expose ourselves to. There are more out there, just take the time and have the integrity to make the right choice in this area.

Don't buy into the lies when it comes to media. I think my view on this has changed as I've matured and spent more time in ministry. Being a dad has also helped that. I've met several youth leaders who have bought into the lie that we have to watch/listen to everything our students do in order to connect with them. I'm not saying that we shouldn't be culturally aware. We absolutely need cultural awareness. I love sites like CPYU.org (Center for Parent and Youth Understanding) because they have a lot of information on culture influences and media items. I recommend it highly. But as a pastor, I've heard others say, "We don't need to watch porn to tell guys why it's a bad idea." I don't want to sit here and write a list of what is good and what is bad because we all have to make that choice on our own. However, what we watch/listen to affects who we are and our own spiritual walks. We need to make wise choices about those things. Recently I had a local youth volunteer tell me that he took his wife to see *We Are the Millers*. He said it was hilarious. He really liked it. He said he saw a good number of students there, and he was glad that they saw him because it showed that he wanted to "live in their world." I asked a few questions about whether he thought that was healthy or not, and he became agitated. I was curious about how watching a movie about drug runners, the main actress doing a strip tease, and consistent crude and raunchy humor was going to benefit his ministry. Now that's his choice. I don't know his heart and don't want to question it. However, I don't see any benefit in that decision, especially because even secular reviews told us those behaviors would be in the movie. My bigger concern was the damage he could have been done to his students when they saw him there. I thought, *What's going to happen when he teaches on purity? What are they going to say when he tells them not to watch a certain type of movie?* I think it would be hard for him to take a stand on those things after this incident. It's not impossible, just a little more challenging.

I have a certain standard for the media I choose—both what I personally take in and what I teach to students. Am I perfect? Absolutely not. But I think we should be careful about what we take in visually, lyrically, thematically, etc. I believe wholeheartedly that we should not let ourselves be tricked into thinking that by limiting what media we participate in will limit our effectiveness in ministry. Our effectiveness will be found in the fact that we love, invest in, and reach out to the students in our church, not what we listen to, what we watch, how we dress, or how we cut our hair.

Do *not* compromise boundaries. This is a bit different than what I previously mentioned about being their friends. What I'm referring to here has more to do with leader-student boundaries. It is so important for us to *never* blur this line. In the past we've always been more concerned with gender boundaries—male leaders only meeting with male students and female leaders with female students. However, as the years have gone on, it's become less and less about gender and more and more about leader-student boundaries overall. It's no longer prudent to only worry about male leaders meeting with female students and vice versa. As unfortunate incidents have occurred over the recent years, it's become more and more necessary to expand those boundaries over all adult-student relationships. How can we best do this?

Never be alone with a student in private *at all!* While privacy for teens is necessary if they're going to trust you, you must protect them and yourself. Never meet with any student in a private area alone—not your office, not your home, nowhere. If a student needs to meet with you one-on-one, meet him or her in public. If you must meet at the church building, sit out in the open where everyone can walk. If the person agrees to it, meet at a local coffee shop, fast-food place, donut shop, etc. Meet somewhere there are witnesses and accountability. It will serve to protect you against false accusations.

If you meet a student somewhere in public for a one-on-one conversation, please make sure that student's parents know. You don't have to tell the parents why you're meeting with the student or the details of what he or she says. But making sure they know you're meeting the student protects you from a false accusation.

Be appropriate with physical touch. There are times when students in the midst of a crisis, emergency, or emotional meltdown need a hug. If there are witnesses, a side hug may be appropriate. Avoid full frontal hugs as much as possible. We all know that there are times when students surprise you with a full-on hug. If you can avoid full hugs, you should. But in that case, make it quick and move on. Again, this is for your protection. On normal days high-fives and pats on the back are always great! They communicate care without blurring lines.

Keep texting/e-mail on appropriate levels. For example, we shouldn't be texting a student late into the evening (unless it's a crisis) or messaging about your extremely personal matters. We shouldn't be sharing with students any type of marital/relationship issues, fights at home, problems with our kids, or personal struggles we're going through. Sometimes some of those can be great teaching illustrations once they're resolved and we have family permission. Communicating late at night or talking about intensely personal things can create an unhealthy intimacy, and that can lead to bigger trouble.

As leaders, it's so important for us to keep these boundaries tight and solid in order to protect ourselves as the leaders and to protect them as people who trust you.

These boundaries also include how much time you spend doing ministry with ministry people. Don't get me wrong. Ministry is awesome! What else can we do that is better than serving the Lord? However, we have to remember that anything that consumes us can be just as unhealthy as any sin we encounter. We need to make sure the boundaries we set are also for our own health.

If we have a family, we need to make sure they know that they're your top priority. If we're spending too much time in ministry, we can lose our families. And that is something Jesus *never* asked from us. Our families should be our top ministry, and we should make sure that everyone knows that. We also need to set boundaries to make sure we're taking care of ourselves mentally, emotionally, and physically. We can't do that and spend every free moment with students.

If you are single, you still need to set those boundaries both for yourself and for your future family. If you set tight boundaries now, when a family comes into the picture, you'll be good to go!

Never allow yourself to believe that you're *just* a youth minister. We are youth ministers! We aren't *just* anything! Don't sell yourself short. As I stated previously, we cannot think of student ministry as a lesser ministry. We cannot allow others to see student ministry as lesser. If we are going to accomplish that, then we cannot allow anyone to convince us that because we serve with students, our role is lesser than anyone else on staff. Over the years I've seen places where student pastors are treated as if they're on the same level as the custodial staff. I joke about it now and have some fun with it, but the reality is that we can sell ourselves short and allow our role to seem lesser when we shouldn't. If you're on staff at a church or if you are a volunteer, you're fulfilling a tremendous role in a ministry that isn't for everyone. If we start using the word *just*, then we will start leading and ministering on a lesser level because we will have set the bar low. If we want people to see our ministries as legit and a huge part of our overall church's health, then we have to see ourselves as legitimate ministers and part of the overall church team.

I'll end this chapter by sharing the opening quote from John Maxwell again. "Leadership is not about titles, positions or flowcharts. It is about one life influencing another."

There are lots of things that leaders are called up to do and not do. Sometimes they seem unfair or at least out of the ordinary. Sometimes they'll pull us out of our comfort zones, and sometimes they'll be in our sweet spot. But no matter what these are, we need to be leaders in our ministries.

Remember, we don't lead through our title. We cannot bank on our title of leader/pastor/director being our leadership identity. At the end of the day, people don't care what we're called. They care about the impact we have. Not many of us got into this ministry for the glory or the honor it comes with. We chose this ministry because above all things, we want to impact the next generation. We want to build into those who will in turn potentially build into our future kids.

This role of student ministry pastor/leader/director can be an amazing one. I often tell people that I truly believe that I have the best job in the world! And I truly mean it! I have a job that gives me the greatest opportunity to impact and change the world around me. Most people say that they want to change the world, but few ever really get to. In student ministry we get to do it every weekend. We get to do it with every phone call, text, conversation, and coffee we share with our students. We're not just accomplishing a task but building into people. Those people someday will become pastors, CEOs, local politicians, parachurch leaders, and maybe even president—all roles where they can actually enact change. We get to be a part of that!

What role could be better?

Chapter 7

Time Management

> We live and we die by time, and we must not commit the sin of turning our back on time.
> —Chuck Noland (Tom Hanks) in *Cast Away* (2000)

> Making the best use of time, because the days are evil.
> —Ephesians 5:16 (ESV)

> So, whether you eat or drink, or whatever you do, do all to the glory of God.
> —1 Corinthians 10:31 (ESV)

Time management is not every youth leader's best friend. Some of us excel at it, and some of us don't. (I fall into the second category.) Each of us needs to be mindful of our time because it's one thing that we cannot stop, change, or get back. As each second passes, we can't get it back.

Tom Hanks is one of my favorite actors of all time. I love the movie *Cast Away*. Hanks plays Chuck Noland, an operations specialist for FedEx. The movie reveals that his job is to evaluate the processes of FedEx hubs around the world, which leads him on his disastrous adventure when he's stranded after a plane crash. As the movie opens, it cuts to a scene with Chuck in Russia. He mailed a package to himself there to prove that the location was taking too much time to deliver packages. As he's speaking, he's tells the Russian workers, "We live and die by time, and we must not commit the sin of turning our back on time."

Noland is obsessed with time. Everything is his life is ruled by time—his relationship, his work, his goals. He lives with a beeper, and he won't allow himself to not think about time. While many of us are not this obsessed with time, we do need to take it seriously. Scripture warns us in Ephesians 5 that we should be "making the best use of time, because the days are evil." It reminds us that each day is stealing time from us, so we need to make the best use of it. As 1 Corinthians tells us, whatever we do, we must do it for God's glory. Do you know what that means? It means we need to fill our time with things that glorify God, and that means that we cannot waste our time. We cannot find ourselves letting days slip away, filled with things that don't matter, things that aren't worthy of God's time.

Does that mean we can't have downtime? Absolutely not! We need downtime! As we addressed in the last chapter, we need to build margins and boundaries so we can make room for downtime. We need to rest. We need solitude. We need time with just us and the Lord. We need time for family and friendships. We need time to make sure we have a balanced lifestyle. Ministry has a high rate of burnout. If we're not careful, we can be consumed by ministry. We may always be returning that one more phone call before going home, listening to one more story after a ministry event, and attending one more student game before heading to a personal commitment. It can happen so easily. However, we need to recognize the difference between downtime and laziness. Downtime is time to unwind, time to recharge. Laziness is just wasting time, waiting for the next event to occur. It's a world of difference! Playing video games (even as an adult) isn't wrong! I enjoy playing sports games to unwind. So playing for an hour or two once a week (maybe twice at max) is unwinding. Playing the game ten to twelve hours a day multiple days a week and foregoing other life demands is laziness. It's so important that we make sure we delineate the difference. Scripture has an awesome verse that applies to this concept. Proverbs 16:27–29 (TLB) reminds us that "idle hands are the devil's workshop." This reminds us that when we're not doing something, we'll get into trouble. King David is a great example of this. We read about this in 2 Samuel 11 (ESV), which says, "In the spring of the year, the time when kings go out to battle, David sent Joab, and his servants with him, and all Israel. And they ravaged the Ammonites and besieged Rabbah. But David remained at Jerusalem." David was the mighty king handpicked by God, known as a man "after God's own heart" (Acts 13:22). He was the man who was leading Israel, and he should have been leading them into war at this time. However, in a dangerous fashion, he stayed home and sent someone else in his place. Why is this dangerous? Check out what happens next.

In 2 Samuel 11:2–5, we read,

> It happened, late one afternoon, when David arose from his couch and was walking on the roof of the king's house, that he saw from the roof a woman bathing; and the woman was very beautiful. And David sent and inquired about the woman. And one said, "Is not this Bathsheba, the daughter of Eliam, the wife of Uriah the Hittite?" So David sent messengers and took her, and she came to him, and he lay with her. (Now she had been purifying herself from her uncleanness.) Then she returned to her house. 5 And the woman conceived, and she sent and told David, "I am pregnant."

Now we can find several things wrong with this. David had an affair with a married woman and got her pregnant. As we keep reading, we go on to discover that he sent her husband to the front line of battle to cover up the affair. He essentially gets her husband murdered. But before he does that, he brings him in to the castle, gets him drunk, and tries to send him home to be with his wife, probably hoping that if they were intimate, the baby would be seen as theirs. Yet Uriah, Bathsheba's husband, would not do that. He was dedicated to being with his troops and would not leave the king's house. This sounds like something out of our current culture, maybe a top reality show. However, this is a true story. Where did a man like David go wrong?

Was it looking at Bathsheba bathing naked on her roof? Well, that wasn't the best judgment. Was it sending for her, knowing she was married, and sleeping with her? That wasn't the best use of wisdom either. Maybe it was trying to cover it up in different ways, ultimately ending with a killing? Nope. It went bad in verse 1 when the kings went off to war. David did *not* fulfill his calling and go with them. He stayed home with his backside on the couch (and yes, the Bible actually says he got up from the couch). He had idle hands. See what happened. Trouble arose, and sin got the best of the man "after God's own heart."

We're no different. Just because we are ministers, that doesn't mean we are invincible. We can fall to sin because we're human. When we allow downtime to become too much, we can find ourselves in the same position. Maybe our Bathsheba isn't a woman. Maybe it's gossip and discord that we'll find ourselves embroiled by when we're not where God wants us to be. Maybe it is a sexual sin. Perhaps we'll find ourselves online venturing onto inappropriate sites because of boredom. Maybe we just commit the sin of sitting around and wasting time.

We have to be wise about the fine line between downtime and laziness.

Where do we start managing our time?

It all starts with one word—*prioritize!*

Listen. We can all get busy. It's easy to get busy. It's easy to go home at night and be exhausted from a long day at work. It's easy to fill calendar slots with appointments, meetings, projects, and trips. We can certainly do enough to show the church that our ministry has a lot going on. However, that's not what we're called to do. We can be busy cooking onion rings at Burger King. We need to take what time we have and be intentional with it. We need to prioritize our time so that we're not allowing ourselves to be ruled by the calendar. Instead we need to make the calendar a tool for us.

How do we start prioritizing our time?

First, ask yourself, "What's the most important thing my life?" If you answered music, movies, your Xbox, your Pokémon collection, your iPad, your sound system, or anything other than Jesus Christ, then you've already built your foundation to fail. I'm not judging anyone's heart, for that's not my place. But Jesus Christ is to always be our first love (Revelation 2:4). If He isn't, then anything we do in our ministries is done out of the wrong heart. Yes, we might want to help people, and that's not bad. But Jesus didn't die for us to be helpful. He died for our sins so we could extend forgiveness, and He calls for us to share that message with others. If that doesn't drive us, if we're not so in love with Jesus Christ that our entire focus is serving Him, then we shouldn't be in ministry. If you're reading this and you're heading into ministry, please hear my heart when I say this: If you're not sold on Jesus first (not a philosophy, not a popular author, not a liberal social justice cause), please don't pursue ministry. Jesus Christ should always be our top priority in all part of our lives. Plain and simple.

Secondly, what about your family and personal time? What do you need to do to keep balance? If you are single, your life will look different from others who have spouses and families. Either way, you need to take time for yourself. This isn't selfish. It's about achieving a life balance. It will help you avoid burnout. This time includes many things.

Get enough sleep! Sleep is a natural thing in any ministry, but it seems to be more important in student ministry. Yes, you have trips and retreats where sleep is optional. But there is also the fact that a lot of student ministry happens after hours. Students don't just have crises between the hours of 9:00 a.m. and 5:00 p.m. Well, no one does. However, with most adults, they understand if we cannot speak to them at midnight. They understand if we pray with them and ask to meet them first thing the next morning. Most of them understand how a good night's rest will help you sort things in the morning. Teens don't. When they experience crises, they generally need attention right away. It's not that they are intentionally waiting until late at night. They're simply at a stage of life when they're not quite ready to process many of the situations they find themselves in. While we need to be available, we need to make sure we're protecting our rest time. Not getting enough sleep on a regular basis can lead to emotional, mental, and physical breakdowns, none of which helps you or your ministry.

Eat right and exercise! This is one that I'm working on changing in my personal life. I'm starting to realize that diet and exercise impacts ministry more than I ever knew. Years of eating pizza, drinking soda, and staying up late nights catch up with you after a while. In my twenties I did that and rebounded like a champ. Now I'm forty, and a late night of pizza and soda with students causes me to wake up feeling like I was beaten down by a champ. I've gone to a gym off and on over the past couple of years, and I can notice a huge difference in my life. When I go, I feel great. When I don't, I feel subpar. Make sure to take care of yourself however you see fit. You may want to go vegan, try only organic, or do portion control—whatever. Find a diet and exercise plan that works for you.

Keep hobbies and have fun! What are you into? Sports? Reading? Art? Find time to do the things you enjoy doing. It helps keep you balanced and focused. It also provides a great stress relief. It gives you a time and place to not think about ministry. I'm a huge sports fan! I'm a big Cleveland sports fan. It's what I grew up on. Living in the Northeast, I don't get to see my teams play live a lot. So when they're on television, I'll carve out a couple of hours to sit and watch. Does watching my teams help me be a better pastor? Nope! At least not directly. However, once that game is over, I feel a bit mentally refreshed, and I can work on things with a little more clarity. I also enjoy reading, especially leadership and history books. I've found that reading relaxes me and helps me get a clearer view on life. I don't feel ashamed to spend time doing those things, watching movies, or playing games. Each of us in ministry needs those kinds of outlets.

What about family obligations? If you're single, this section includes parents and siblings. If you're married with kids, they should take the higher priority. Ministry won't mean anything if you lose your family in the process. In calling us to ministry, Jesus never meant for us to put our roles above our wives and kids. Divorce is not foreign to churches and ministers. Many people think that pastors and ministers have it all together. They think that our families and marriages are always healthy because we're serving God after all! He'll always make sure we're taken care of. Unfortunately that's not even close to the truth. In fact, because we are serving God, our marriages and families are the main place Satan attacks us. If he can hurt those close to us, he can get to us. Our family obligations should come first, and then comes our commitment to our walk with Jesus. Our families should never feel like they take a backseat to our ministry. Our families are our first ministry field. If we lose them, how can we reach others?

Here's how my personal priority chart looks.

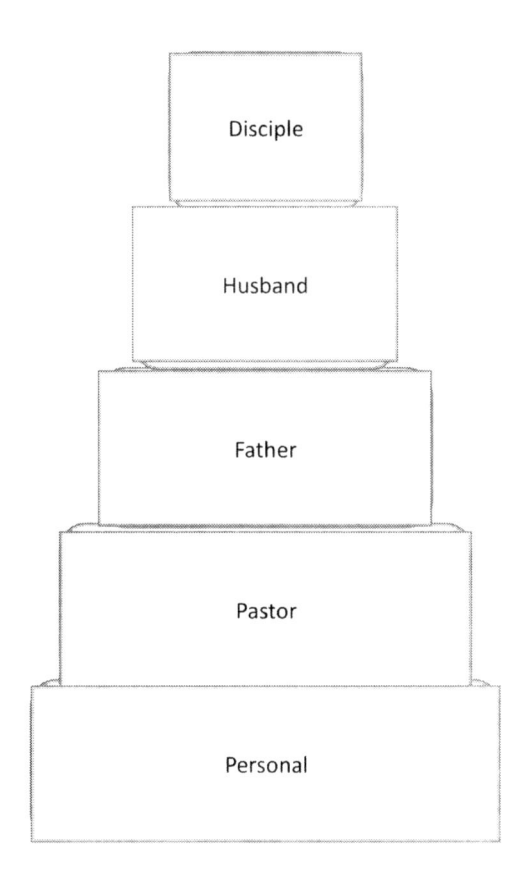

- Disciple
- Husband
- Father
- Pastor
- Personal

How do I prioritize my ministry time?

I can't tell you how to prioritize your personal time. I've shared my thoughts in this chapter, but since I don't know each of you, it would presumptuous for me to tell you how to divide up your free time. I included my priority pyramid here just to share how I split things up. Hopefully it's helpful.

I believe we can all learn from one another about how to prioritize our ministry time. Before we go into the details, let's talk logistics.

The most important thing I've learned is to keep a detailed calendar. It's extremely helpful to keep details straight. As I said before, you shouldn't let the calendar control you. It's a tool to help keep your ministry organized. It's a tool to keep you organized. If you're a paper person, At-A-Glance are the best organizers out there in my opinion. I've used them since college. They're well laid out with plenty of options, and they are very cost efficient. If you're an electronics person or live by your phone, apps like Evernote can be amazingly helpful. For apps, I also recommend using Dropbox (to manage and send files) and OneNote to organize notebooks and notes as well. However, with all of the options out there, I would highly recommend that you commit to keep *one* calendar. I say this because in our day and age, people can trick themselves into thinking that the more calendars they have, the less chance they'll forget something. Unfortunately this can have the opposite effect. If we try to live by our calendar/organizing app and a separate paper calendar, we may find ourselves making an appointment on one without updating the other. Living by one calendar keeps you centered on one and makes it less likely that you'll double-book an appointment or forget one because the calendar you have wasn't the one you used to make it.

Keep one calendar. Choose the one that works best for you and stick to it. It may be a little annoying at times to keep everything straight, but it will save a great amount of stress in the long run.

Okay, let's get back to the day-to-day prioritizing.

First thing to figure out is what church or ministry meetings are you committed to attending during an average week? I'm referring to meetings or events that you're required to be at, such as staff meetings, team meetings, trainings, and any other requirements for your particular role. I would also include weekend requirements—church services, Sunday school, student worship services, and anything else that you have to be at. Write those down, and tally up the amount of hours those take. Again, don't become ruled by the clock; however, those are things that you need to be at, and they're probably nonnegotiable.

Secondly, when are your main student ministry meetings? Youth groups? Small groups? Those are things you should be at and participate in. Obviously you can't attend everything, but it's good to know what meets when. Which ones are you expected to lead and/or teach at?

Third, estimate how much office time you need per week for phone calls, e-mails, admin work, leadership prep, and training and message prep. Remember, the more ministry events or groups you need to be a part of, the more prep time you'll need. As you go through this process, you may feel the need for an admin assistant (if one isn't already on staff). It's helped me to actually calendar my prep time and office time so I make sure that I keep that time carved out.

Lastly you need to build in margins, meaning time slots that exist for the accidental things that pop up (e.g., the emergency calls, the student who wants to meet for coffee to talk, the time the guys stop by to play basketball, the moments that we cannot plan for). One thing that I've found that can drive a wedge between you and your students (or their parents) is being too busy to be there when they need you. If you ask any veteran pastor (especially youth pastors), they will tell you that congregation members can have unrealistic expectations of their ministry leaders. People in crisis rarely understand that you may have things already going on.

When they're in crisis, they want attention. There are times when your attention is needed ASAP. Building in margins will help you attend to those people without feeling like another commitment has to be adjusted.

Along with work margins, make sure to build margins in for personal time as well. We can be consumed by ministry if we let ourselves. Make sure to build in margins for impromptu lunch dates with your significant others or your own kids. Build in margins to take in a movie or indulge in some personal reading or even take a nap! It's important to your overall life balance and health.

Time management is something that is vital for all of us. Before you enter into ministry, take an inventory of how you currently manage your time. If you're in school, how are you organizing your life? If you're changing careers, are there areas in your time management that you need to tweak? Regardless of where you're coming from, take the time to figure this out. It will go a long way toward keeping your ministry and your personal life balanced and healthy.

Chapter 8

The Weekend Date

The most fun and possibly the more stressful part of finding the right ministry position is the interview, and potential interviewing weekend. In the past I've heard this time referred to as the "weekend date." It's a funny title, but it ends up being a very accurate description.

We've all been on first dates before, right? We're nervous during them. We're looking for a fun time with the other person. But we can also be nervous because we can find ourselves worrying that the other person will not like us. Are we dressed okay? Did we pick the right place to go? How do we say good night? What do we talk about? What if it goes really badly really early? How do we deal with that? Do I have enough money with me? What if they're allergic to the food at the restaurant? What if I'm allergic to the food at the restaurant? What if I drop my glass of water on the table, make a huge mess, and then spill the large pitcher on their lap while they try to clean the mess up? (Don't laugh. That happened to me once.) We can go through a number of different scenarios in our heads, most of which have us ending the night in a disaster. This doesn't mean we're negative people, but I think that it's quite normal that we tend to worry about the unknown.

Just like a first date with the girl or guy we find attractive can be unnerving, so can beginning the weekend date with a church where we are interested in serving. Like any first date, the weekend is very much a time to put your best foot forward. And the church will too. Both of you are looking for a potential marriage. They're bringing you in because what they know of you interests them. And you've accepted their invitation because what you know of them interests you. Nothing is a done deal yet, but it's certainly a very positive step. However, I (and many other friends of mine) have had rough experiences on these weekends. Not because the churches weren't amazingly accommodating but because we weren't prepared. We didn't know what exactly to ask and what exactly to share. Overall, many of these have worked out just fine.

What should I be aware of?

Obviously, while we are going through this weekend, we should be keeping our eyes and ears open to the things that aren't in the conversations. I know that this may sound weird, but hang with me.

One the greatest things I've learned in ministry is the ability to just be aware. That may sound like a new-age thought, but I'm not talking about looking for some mystic power. I'm talking about just noticing what is going around us. The culture of the church and the core of what they're about can be seen by just walking through and noticing things.

For example, when you walk the halls, does the church use bulletin boards? If so, how are they decorated? Paper boarders and clip art may reveal that the church isn't current or culturally connected.

So You Want to be in Youth Ministry?

How prominent is technology in the church, not just in the worship center or sanctuary but throughout the church? We live in a technological age. Each generation coming up is becoming more and more tech-savvy. Does the church show signs of understanding this development and their goals to incorporate technology into the church?

Does the building look like it's appealing to a younger generation, or does it look like it's an aged building with no sign of a youthful influence? I am not talking about architecture or carpet colors, because many of those things are unchangeable or at least carry a heavy cost to change. If it's a smaller church, these things may be bound by income. Look at the kids and student ministry spaces. Are they multifunctional or age-specific? If they are multifunctional spaces, how are they divided and scheduled out? The answers to these questions will give you insights into the overall church vision for student ministry.

Paul mentions similar things like these in 1 Corinthians 9:22–23 (ESV) when he says "I have become all things to all people that by all means I might save some. I do it all for the sake of the gospel, that I may share with them in its blessings." I don't believe that we have to incorporate every piece of our culture in order to reach people. However, it's vital for the church to understand the culture it exists in. And it's vital that we find ways to use that culture for the glory of Christ. As I said in a previous chapter, we don't have to watch every movie to be able to reach students. We do need to at least understand what they are about so we can be wise. Scripture calls us to be wise. There are several books about the importance of wisdom. It's important that we connect with the world we are trying to reach. There are studies that actually say that a new visitor will decide whether or not to attend your church within several seconds of being on your campus. That means visitors could decide not to attend your church if your landscaping isn't appealing or if the parking lot looks crowded or if the area isn't easy to access. It sounds crazy, but it can happen. Once they're inside of our church buildings, they feel connected. They feel welcomed, and when they look around, they can see that the church is a place that is dedicated to reaching those around them.

If we are using VCRs, if our bulletin boards look like a first-grade classroom from a decade ago, or if our ministry spaces seems disheveled and unorganized, then we can give the impression of a church that isn't moving forward.

Keep your ears open as well!

I'll share with you one of my "red flag" statements. This is just for me, so please don't hear this as something that can happen everywhere. But when I've interviewed with churches or ministries, if I heard the phrase "We're committed to reaching the young people," I would get worried. The words *young people* conjure up images of grandparents giving compliments while they're drinking cups of tea and sitting in their living room with paisley wallpaper. I know that sounds judgmental, and I don't mean it to be; however, I want to be honest.

Listening for those phrases will give you an idea about where their thinking is. I once interviewed at a church that routinely and consistently told me that they wanted to reach the next generation (teens and young adults) and wanted to reach the community. However, once we began, it became evident that their definition of those things and mine were very different. I don't say that to imply that anyone was dishonest. I don't think that at all. I think that they just had a different view of doing that than I did. And instead of making for a tighter fit, it created a little rift in vision.

As you're talking with people, interviewing with leaders, and getting to know those you may be working with, keep your ears open so you can really hear what they're saying, and more importantly, listen to what they're not saying. Many times on these weekends, they want to share the best views of themselves. After all, they're sharing their greatest desires for ministry.

Here are some things to listen for. Will you be responsible for things outside your ministry? Or will you be specifically focused on students/teens. Make sure that's clear. Be careful of any statements that say you'll be serving in "any other ways as needed" or something along those lines. That's not to say that we shouldn't serve in other ways and others ministries. However, if that's not made clear up front, it can make things sticky.

Are there any expectations or responsibilities (officially or unofficially) for your spouse? It's not uncommon for churches to expect ministry spouses to do certain things, attend certain events, or be involved in certain ministries. It's not always right, but the expectations can exist.

What are the current ministry leaders saying about the role you're interviewing for? What are they saying about your predecessor? What are they saying about church leadership? Again, be mindful of what they're not saying. Not to chase gossip, but people will tend not to tell you the behind-the-scene secrets during this time because they won't want to push you away, and they truly won't want to talk ill of the past. Many may be willing to let the past be the past, and they may want to move forward, possibly with you as their leader.

Years ago I was interviewing with a church for a part-time role as a possible internship. As we were going through the weekend date, people were incredibly friendly. I began asking about the ministry's history, and the leaders immediately got quiet. They shared with me the different tasks and events they did. They even shared some stories about a couple of the students. What I noticed was that they said nothing about my predecessor—good or bad. At first I didn't think much about it, but as I thought about it, I began to realize that they didn't answer any of my questions about him. It was an instance when their lack of words told me more than anything they actually said. I did not end up taking the role with them because of their needs and my schedule for school. However, I did run into one of those leaders a year later in a seminary class, and he shared with me that former youth pastor left contentiously and that no one wanted to say anything bad about him. I admired their heart in protecting their former leader, and I know that it's hard to share information like that. However, their silence spoke volumes to me.

What's the body language of everyone like? Do people genuinely seem excited about you, the interview, and the church? When you talk about your vision for then ministry, watch people's postures. Are they excited and leaning in to hear more? Or do they slouch back and fold their arms, seemingly detached from what you're saying? How much do people want to talk with you and get to know you, and how much do they just want to hear you and move on? Even if they say they're glad you are there, watch the body language. That will tell you so much. Negative reactions aren't necessarily about you. For some, change is hard, and their reaction may involve their perception of what is happening. For others, their relationship with the former leader may have them upset. As humans, it's hard not to show our emotions. I know some can be stone-faced and unflappable, and that can be a gift. For the majority, we show our emotions through our reactions and body language. If we can learn to read those reactions, it can help us control our emotions.

This weekend date can be a lot of fun ... and a lot of work.

What's the best way to prepare for this type of weekend?

As you prep for this weekend, there are a few practical things you can do to get yourself ready. The first one is obvious but extraordinarily vital. Ready for it? Here it is—*pray!*

It's so important to prepare for the weekend in prayer. Prayer should be central to our entire lives anyway, but if we're honest with ourselves, we have slipups. We have days when our schedules, exhaustion, or illnesses can deter us from prayer. It's not that we're not dedicated, but we let our human sides take over. For this weekend prayer needs to be a focus because this is a life-altering weekend—regardless of the outcome! If it works out, most likely you'll be beginning another ministry chapter in your life. If it doesn't, you'll at least know that the door is closed, and you can begin your search for the next chapter. Either way, the outcome doesn't alter things.

After praying, prep your best message. Not the one that makes you sound like the smartest, the funniest, or the ideal leader. Prep the best message that gives everyone the best idea of who you are, what you're passionate about, and what they'll get if you end up there. Too many times I've seen potential youth leaders put together flawless, impeccable messages and wow both the students and church leaders, but when they arrive, there is a letdown. The messages become more mediocre to the students, and the impact is viewed as lacking. Sadly it may have nothing to do with the new youth pastor's teaching style. He may just have set the bar too high on his interviewing weekend. You don't solve that by giving a half effort in your message prep. However, it does remind us of how important it is for us to make sure what we preach is backed up and illustrated in our daily lives. If people see that in your message during this weekend, then they'll feel like they can connect with you personally. That will go a long way.

When you are booking your travel, try to make sure to give yourself plenty of time to relax, unwind, and not rush from place to place. If you're first meeting is at 1:00 p.m., don't arrive in town at 12:45 p.m., even if the church is close. Give yourself a chance to get into town, have a bite to eat, sit down, take a deep breath, and change your clothes—whatever you can do to relax for a few minutes before you enter into the process. Years ago I was interviewing at a church down south. They were awesome about arranging and paying for all of my travel costs. However, in order to get the best rate they could, they booked me a flight that arrived at the airport an hour before my first meeting. The airport thankfully was only ten miles from the church and twelve miles from my hotel, so I didn't see much of an issue. But as is normal with travel, the flight landed ten minutes late. The bags took longer to get to baggage claim than usual. My rental car wasn't ready, and there was construction. I was in a foreign city and didn't know my way around, so I couldn't take a detour. Although my flight was scheduled to land an hour before my meeting, I ended up being twenty minutes late, and I wasn't able to check into my hotel until later that night. In the big picture, those are just nuisances. However, I felt it got us off on the wrong foot for the entire weekend and changed the perspective. The role wasn't for me in the end, but I learned a valuable lesson. *Give yourself time!*

Pull your vision portfolio together. I've met people with differing views on this. Some say it's good. Some say it's a waste of time. In my mind, pulling together a portfolio of ministry can't be a bad thing. Pull together some details from past ministry events, your own ministry vision and goals, and any resources you feel have helped you get to where you're at. The church leaders may ask you for them, or they may not. I always have found that having that info ready shows initiative and desire. I've had a few churches tell me these things weren't necessary. However, I had a few that said that packet of information helped them see my vision and understand my heart after the weekend was done. It's another tool to help communicate who you are. It may even be a resource a church might ask for before the weekend happens.

Make sure to check out their website (if they have one). How does it look? How easy is it to navigate? What's the verbiage that they use? As I mentioned previously, these things will give you a great insight into many of the things that they won't say. Again, it's hard to believe a church is committed to reaching the world they currently live in if their site is full of muted colors and clip art.

Lastly, research the area where you're interviewing. I can't tell you how many young guys and girls I've spoken to who never thought of doing this. By research, I mean real research, not just finding out where things are and how many Chick-fil-A's there are in town. Read about the area's history, its demographics, and its culture. Learn about their sports teams and how crazy their fans are. Look around where the schools are and find out where they are ranked educationally. Find out about local customs. I say this because it will help you as you prep for this weekend date. It's all info you can weave into conversations over the weekend. These details will serve as great conversation starters, but they will also show people that you're seriously interested in the role.

What kinds of questions should I ask?

This is one area where I wish I had received more coaching. I tended to go through a weekend like this, listen as much as I could, and notice as much as I could, but then when it came to ask questions, I would come up empty! I would think of questions on the way home or in my hotel room later in the day when the interview process was over. Few questions would have mattered in the long run, but there were a few answers I think may have changed my view of the role. I'll go back to what my teachers in elementary school always told me. The only stupid question is the unasked one. What should we ask?

It's okay to ask about salary! Yes, this is a ministry opportunity. However, it's still a job. You still need to provide for yourself and possibly a family. In most of these weekends, the salary discussion happens toward the end. So don't worry if it doesn't come up in the first set of discussions. In my experience the salary package is discussed when the leadership is comfortable about offering you the role. It doesn't always go that way, but in my experience this is how it happens for the majority of the time. But don't be afraid to ask about it or about benefits and perks in the compensation package. Don't be afraid to talk openly about it, especially if it becomes a hindrance to you taking the position. I know that churches or ministries have limited resources. I believe that the package they're offering has been discussed, prayed over, and decided on as a fair package. However, I don't believe God wants us to make any decision based solely on money. He wants us to make decisions based on His leading and His guidance. If the salary package is one that we don't think we can live on or take care of a family on, we need to say something! What is the worst thing that could happen? The church says that they're sorry and that's the max that they can offer? Is that so bad? If that happens, we can at least talk and pray about it with all of the details laid out. In the best-case scenario, we open a dialogue about the package and see if there is any room for change. It's all healthy! Please don't read this and think that I condone salary negotiations. We're not professional athletes who can hold out for more money. We're not free agents who can play one church against another. We're leaders who need to make the best decision possible for the church, for our families, for ourselves, and for God's glory.

It's okay—in fact, it's necessary—to ask about the last leader the ministry had. We need to know what we're walking into. There may be a perfect time on the weekend to do this, and it may be a discussion that the leaders voluntarily offer up. However it comes out, you need to know what happened to your predecessor. Maybe we don't need to know every dirty detail, but we need enough so that we're not caught up in a messy situation through no fault of our own! If the previous leader left to pursue another position, that's fine. It's good to know that because it will help you honor his or her legacy and what the minister there has done. That will help you bridge the gap between the past to the present with the students. If the previous leader isn't there anymore because of a contentious split or moral failure, that's good to know too. Many will take their feelings about the former leader out on you. It's not because they blame you but because you're there and the former leader is not. Make sure you have a clear answer about why the position is open currently. If you don't get all of the details, that's okay. However, it's in your best interest to at least find out as much as you can.

Ask about what the church's growth and outreach vision is! Regardless of how they see student ministry fitting into that, you need to know. It gives you a great insight into where they see things going. It will help you see how they see themselves reaching out to the culture around them. Church ministries have to exist in a symbiotic circle. Families will come to a church if they feel comfortable, if the church has good programs for their kids, and if the programs are something they can connect with. Well, if the kids and student ministries aren't healthy and active, families may not stay around. If they don't stay around, the attendance in the worship center will drop. If the worship center attendance drops, then there won't enough volunteers to reach out to families and serve in the children and student ministries. Donations will drop. Staff will get cut, and the church won't have enough resources to turn their situation around. Asking them about their vision for growth shows them you're interested in the church beyond your ministry, and it also shows them that you're not there to entertain kids. You're there to be a minister and to disciple students into the people God wants them to be! We only get students for a few years, and we want to be able to pass them off to a healthy congregation.

Ask how they measure success. Do they use numbers? Do they use the emotional culture of the ministry? If they can't articulate that, then you may find yourself being judged on subjective ideals. Those can change from day to day, depending on mood, stress, ministry challenges, etc. It never ends up positive. Success today may not be judged by the same definition tomorrow. Ask for clear direction on the metrics of ministry success. I'm not saying that any definition is wrong. But it's important to keep your eyes wide open and to know what you're going into. You need to know what you'll be measured up to. We can never accomplish anything unless we know what we are supposed to accomplish. This answer will impact how you minister. Some will measure you on attendance numbers. If so, then you'll have to have an incredibly dedicated outreach and evangelism strategy constantly bringing in new students. If you are measured by the depth of growth of the students, then you're discipleship strategy will be the main piece of your ministry. Neither is bad, but we need to know what it is we are expected to do.

If you are relocating from another area, it's okay to ask if they'll help cover those costs. Moving can be expensive and stressful. Whether you're single or married or you have a family, relocating is upsetting your life to start anew in an unfamiliar place. Be sure to ask if help is available. In my experience the majority of churches will offer some sort of help. In my current position, the church blessed us by paying for professional movers to come and move us. We had to pack everything, but they packed the truck, drove it, and unloaded it. It was a huge help for us as we had two small kids at the time. In my first full-time church position, the church did not help with the moving costs; however, they blessed us by offering to help us unload. They also had a pantry drive for us. (Everyone brought pantry food items to help us stock our pantry to get started.) And they even gave us a small monetary gift. Churches all handle this differently, but remember, your questions aren't demands. They're simply there to make sure you're aware of the details.

Are there things I should avoid doing or saying during this weekend?

Before we go any further, let me say this. I am all for complete honesty and transparency. There should be no question that's off-limits. However, I think there are some things we should be careful to avoid.

Don't go just to go. I have had a couple of instances where my discouragement with other things in life have soured my attitude, thereby affecting my weekend date. It wasn't the fault of the church hosting me, but it was other things in my life that I wasn't mature enough to put aside for forty-eight to seventy-two hours. If you can't go with a correct attitude and reason, then it's best to cancel the weekend rather than go through the motions.

The same applies to the idea of going through this because you need a job. It goes back to the same insulting attitude of doing youth ministry until a "real position" opens up. If a church is willing to host you for the weekend and thinks enough of you to interview you so that you might become a part of their community, you should at least go into it with the right attitude and feel led to do it. If you don't, you're insulting them and the Lord.

I have to admit something. Several years ago I was guilty of doing this. We had left a full-time position, and I was out of work for about six months. I had gotten a call to interview at a church in another state. It was an intriguing position. It sounded like a great opportunity and a chance to build a ministry from the ground up. I honestly went into the weekend date excited about the opportunity. It was in a more rural area than we were used to, but it came with a house to live in for free and a tight-knit community. When we arrived, we were at the church for about forty-five seconds and already had doubts. I began taking notice of things around me. (Remember what I mentioned previously about the nonverbal things that are said?) The church was dated, *very* dated. It had flyers up that had 2002 dates on them. (This was in 2006.). There were faded bulletin boards, broken pews, and kids' equipment that looked dirty. I was trying to remind myself that sometimes money plays into those things. As we walked into the board meeting, it became clear that this wasn't the place for us—not because of looks but because of philosophy. Each question we answered made it clearer that it wasn't a place we could see ourselves. We went back to the hotel. My wife, two kids, and I sat down over pizza. My wife and I tried to find things we connected with, but sadly we couldn't. It wasn't that they weren't wonderful, caring people. It just became clear that we didn't see eye to eye on ministry philosophy. We even discussed calling them that night and saying thanks but no thanks and heading home. After we talked, we decided to stick it out. We wanted to give it a full weekend to see if our minds changed. By the end of Sunday, nothing had changed. In fact, I began to feel guilty. I had already decided in my mind that we weren't coming there, and it affected how I dealt with the weekend. It was completely unfair to the church because they were honestly putting their best foot forward. I felt terrible. When we arrived home, I called the church to say thank you. I told them that while we enjoyed our time with them, we didn't think it was a good fit. I also apologized to the pastor, explaining to him that we felt it wasn't a good fit the first night. I also explained that we even debated going home after the first night and not finishing the weekend. He appreciated the honesty and explanation, and he understood where I was coming from. The worst part was what he said next. He said he could tell how we felt after the first night, and he was expecting us to not finish the weekend. I felt terrible, and I apologized for wasting their time and resources. He was kind, and he shared that while he could tell we didn't feel it was a fit, they really did enjoy hearing our vision for ministry and spending time with us.

We owe it to these churches to go with open minds and hearts. We must ask ourselves, "Is God leading me here?" If we don't, we'll get caught in material things and not the things God could use to change us and them.

Always be yourself. Just keep it in check.

Okay, I'll admit that I can be a goof. I enjoy making people laugh. I crack jokes in counseling sessions and meetings. I'll add funny pictures and stories to sermons (regardless of whether they're for students or adults). I'll play pranks on students, retweet funny statements, and post Facebook memes I think are funny—all in the name of making people laugh. I'm not a comedian, but it's fun to make people laugh. However, there are times when I need to keep that in check. Sometimes you can indeed have too much of a good thing.

Churches bringing you in want to know you—your strengths, your weaknesses, your passions, your hobbies, etc. They genuinely do. I've had no troubles cracking jokes in interviews, but I've been told a couple of times that there is a time to be serious in those meetings. It's not that humor isn't appreciated, but these leadership teams also want to know that we can buckle down and handle the seriousness of others' needs. While there is a time for humor, there is also a time for quiet seriousness. Cracking jokes at birthday parties is great! Cracking them at funerals is not so great. Sharing a humorous story about a student or other church member can be funny. Sharing a story that embarrasses that person isn't.

It's important to have enough self-awareness that we can stop these things before they happen. If we have to be reprimanded for crossing the line, we're not giving a positive impression. While we're all entitled to make a mistake or two, we should know ourselves enough to be careful.

Most importantly, do not talk negatively of your past church roles! This can be hard, especially if you left your last position contentiously. Unfortunately that can happen. When you're on these weekends, people will undoubtedly ask you about your last position. (If this is your first role, keep this in mind for the future.) It's a fine line to share honestly and not avoid negative talk. For some of you reading this, this comes as second nature to you. You've been gifted in this area. For others it takes some work to make sure you share honestly and honorably.

I left a full-time position contentiously. The way things ended were not the way I would have preferred, but they did. It left a bad taste in my mouth and theirs, and it was an overall unhealthy ending. It caused some rifts between a couple of students and me. It also caused a large rift between the students I left and the rest of the church. There were lots of issues that no one outside of leadership knew about, and I didn't share any of those. It was a hurtful time for all involved. It took me several weeks to heal, to forgive, and to ask for forgiveness. When we interviewed at our current church, I was asked several times about our past ministry. I tried very hard to honor the church and leaders I served with, even those I disagreed with. I was told I came across like I was hiding something. Thankfully the senior pastor spoke to district leadership where I last served, and they shared with him what had happened. The district was able to share some details about what had happened, so they got the story, but I was able to honor them in my words and conduct. While it was a tough situation, I learned a lot from that situation. Now it's been several years, and I can talk about it as a learning experience.

It's important to share how our past experiences have impacted us, even if they were negative. But we also cannot blame our past roles for our shortcomings or wounds. At some point we have to own our past issues and the ways we contributed to the negativity of the past. After I left our former church, I blamed them for all of it. As I healed, I began to realize that I played a part in some of the struggles. I realized I could have avoided a lot of issues had I been humble enough to apologize, ask forgiveness, and been more teachable. I was able to apologize to the leadership for my part in things, and I am glad I was able to before I moved on to a new ministry.

Finally, as we wrap up this chapter, let's cover one more thing.

The Offer

At the end of this weekend, there will be an opportunity for a job offer.

If the job is offered, it's easy to accept. We say yes, shake a hand, share a hug, and begin the process of lining up our start date.

If the job is offered and you don't feel it's the right fit, that will be a bit more difficult. It's never easy sharing disappointing news. But it's very important to make sure to be honest but loving. It's important for us to make sure we keep our integrity while we make sure we honor theirs. On this weekend there can be hundreds of reasons that it doesn't work out, and none of them have to do anything wrong with either the church or you. Sometimes it just means that we're not a good fit. And it's okay that it's not a good fit. As we discussed earlier, there are lots of reasons we don't see it as a fit.

In the story I shared earlier, I didn't think the church was a good fit for me. When it came to telling them why I didn't feel it was a good fit, I had to be honest with them. But in being honest, I had to ask myself, "Is it worth it to share every detail with them?" There is a fine line between saying, "Thank you, but I'm going to pass," and sharing everything you didn't like about the role. Doing the latter can come across as inappropriate. While we want to honest, getting too detailed can have an adverse effect.

How do we say no?

First, make sure to be appreciative of the offer. Say thank you. Share your good thoughts and observations from the weekend. Even if you don't see yourself as a good fit there, you certainly can see the good that the church is doing both inside their walls and in their community. Make sure to compliment them and their hospitality for the weekend. Chances are that if they've offered you the role, they're putting themselves out there. It's important that even though you're saying no, they walk away from the weekend encouraged and excited that God still has the right person out there.

Make sure to be honest. As I said previously, be honest. Carefully share with them what you need to. I have seen in the past where people have shared too much, and it's actually insulted the church.

Be careful not to say too much! Let me explain. In some situations it's difficult to deliver bad news. When you have to deliver bad news, you can end up being over complimentary and then digging a hole you can't come out of. It's kind of like a bad break up when a person uses phrases like "It's not you. It's me" or "I need to focus on me now." Those things are said to try to soften the blow. When we say, "No, thank you," to a church's offer, its best that we try to avoid saying those types of phrases. We may not say, "It's not you. It's me," but we can use phrases like "I don't think I'm ready for this challenge" or "Maybe when I have more experience, this would be a great place for me." I think it's good to just shoot straight with them and let your no be no. If we try to "soften the blow," we can end up causing more issues. Churches will understand.

Lastly, say no thanks. Be honest, be straight with them, and say no thanks. Make sure to talk with them in person, or call on the phone at minimum. Don't e-mail. Don't text. It may be easier, but it's completely disrespectful.

This weekend is an incredible opportunity for you, the church, and everyone involved. It's a big step in the process of finding a new ministry opportunity. It's really a make-or-break weekend. I've seen weekends that have gone amazingly! In our current role, we were offered and accepted the job before the weekend was over. It was an awesome weekend together. I have also seen them go incredibly bad. Sometimes the person doesn't get the position, and the same individual also has tainted him or herself for future positions. Word got out about how the weekend went, and churches began to distance themselves.

It's a great weekend! Honor God with it! And most of all, *have fun with it!*

Chapter 9

Now that You've Arrived!

If you're reading this and you've recently accepted a position in student ministry, this chapter is for you! One of the scariest things I've experienced in ministry is that first day. When you walk into the church that first day, you're the youth leader/pastor/director. People will want to give you a bit of time to adjust, but in reality, you have to get moving fairly quickly. In my experience, if you're replacing a leader, there probably is a transition plan in place. If this is a new role and you're the first to occupy it, you'll lay the foundation for the entire ministry going forward.

The most important thing we can do the first day is to meet the staff we are serving with. I love the staff I currently serve with. It doesn't mean that we always see eye to eye or that we always get along. However, there's no doubt that we're on the same page and on the same mission. Over the years I've been able to forge some good friendships with those I serve with. When it comes to ministry, especially church ministry, things can get rough. When those times occur, it's this staff that will be your support system. At times you may feel like you have to circle the wagons together to weather a storm. Spend some time building relationships with this team. Take them to lunch. Have them over for dinner. Spend some time together at events and church services. Cultivate relationships with those you're serving with. It's a necessity for a healthy church dynamic.

Settle In

Don't underestimate the importance of your workspace. When you arrive at your new position, it's important to get yourself settled in. Not every youth ministry staff member has an office space. Some have their own. Some share spaces with others, and some have temporary spaces. Whatever the case is, it's very important to organize and settle into a workspace. Why is it so important? When a chef is about to cook, he lines up the tools he needs before he starts, and the same goes for ministry. No chef wants to stop in the middle of prepping a meal to find a knife he needs or a seasoning he wants. He generally makes sure everything he needs is right there. It helps him do his job swiftly, efficiently, and excellently. For people in roles like ours, it's important that we have our workspaces organized and settled. It's not for appearance sake, but this way we do our jobs efficiently and with excellence. I'm a big believer that how our offices are organized and kept says a lot about us. I can help add credibility to our roles or take away that credibility. Right now my office looks like a storage closet. Admittedly it's messy. However, it's an organized mess. Most of the items stacked up are waiting to be used in our student ministry and children's ministry, or they're waiting to be returned. But if you were to walk in and say hello, you would assume that I'm a disorganized person and person without direction. Once these items are gone, the office will go back to a more organized workspace.

Why is a disorganized and cluttered workspace challenging? It's a constant distraction. It's hard for many to focus when we are among messes. We spend a good amount of our time looking for items we need, moving things around, and possibly even having to clear space to work. If we cannot focus, then we'll find ourselves drifting to and from what we are working on, delivering at best a partially focused effort. That's not excellence. It's barely just good enough. God deserves our best.

It's hard to keep our items straight in a mess. How can we express to others that we have a plan for a ministry dealing with people when our offices and desks look like a bomb went off? When we start losing permission slips, cash and checks, reports to our leaders, and lost-and-found items, we can lose the trust of those we are leading.

We can use the mess as a procrastination tool. We all have days when we don't want to work. Many people have days in their careers when they wake up and just don't feel like going into the office. No matter how much we love our roles, we will have days like this. Some days we can take off, and some days we can't. If our workspaces are messy, then on these days we can convince ourselves to put off the work of ministry for the sake of organizing. While the organizing isn't bad in itself, putting off daily responsibilities to do so can be.

When you arrive in this new role, whatever workspace you are given, take the time to set it up and organize it.

So You Want to be in Youth Ministry?

Here is my organized office.

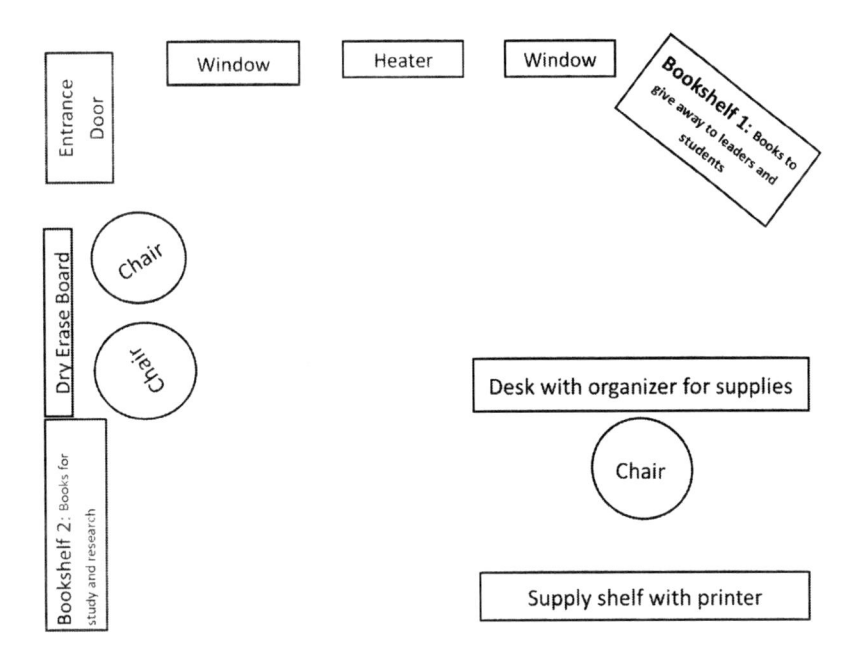

[Office diagram with the following labels: Entrance Door, Window, Heater, Window, Bookshelf 1: Books to give away to leaders and students, Dry Erase Board, Chair, Chair, Bookshelf 2: Books for study and research, Desk with organizer for supplies, Chair, Supply shelf with printer]

There is a method to what goes where. The bookshelf (the giveaway shelf) is the first thing you see when you walk in. That makes it easy to guide people to it, and it shows that our ministry really is interested in giving resources away to help. I placed my desk where it is for two reasons. I didn't want anyone to sneak up on me. Believe it or not, I can tune people out, so it's easy to sneak up on me. Now I can see people walking in to see me. Secondly, when people come in and see me facing the door, it creates a welcoming atmosphere. I've always felt that when you walk into a room and the people in there have their backs to you, it feels a little awkward. The chairs for my guests are on the wall to the left of my desk for a reason. I am not a fan of putting those chairs in front of the desk. I believe that it can give someone a position of power, a commanding position. The desk becomes a barrier between you and those you're speaking to. I believe that the last thing people want when they're talking to their pastor is a barrier. I place the chairs to the left so that when I have someone in to talk, I can roll my chair out, and then we're sitting face-to-face. It helps lower any tension levels, which is great if the conversation is more of a confrontational discussion. The dry-erase board to the left is also strategic. If I'm meeting with my team, I can easily turn the chairs around and have the board available. More importantly, as I'm planning, having it on the left makes it easy for me to see from my desk. I don't have to angle my neck in a painful way to see it on the right wall next to the desk. I have a clean line of sight to what I'm working on without having to have several pads of papers on my lap and desk. The same goes with my second bookshelf with the study books. It's directly next to me so I can read the titles and find what I need. Behind me is a small shelf with supplies on it. If I need Post-it notes, pens, tape, or anything else, it's a small spin around. I don't have to get up and search for stuff.

All in all, organize your workspace so it's effective, strategic, and easy-to-use.

I would also say that while you are settling in to your new workspace, make sure it's personal. By personal, I mean you should make sure that when people are in there, they see parts of who you are. In ministry, no one wants to come into their pastor's office and feel like you're in a lawyer's office or a doctor's office. They want to connect with you and feel like you're a real person. I believe having personal items out and about will help people coming in identify with you and part of who you are. In my office, when you walk in, the first thing you see are four posters for some of my favorite movies—*Jaws, Ghostbusters, Star Wars,* and *Back to the Future.* I have a couple of canvases signed by students from the ministry past, a couple of glass organization boards that double as a dry-erase wall calendar, and a few pictures. On a couple of wall shelves, I have some inspirational sayings in frames, some sports memorabilia of my favorite teams (the Cleveland Browns, Indians, and Cavaliers), a few silly gifts from students, pictures of my kids, and a few other personal trinkets. When people come in and take a look around, I believe they get a small glimpse into who I am and what I enjoy.

I had a man come in to speak to me about a personal issue, an issue he was a little embarrassed about. As he sat down, he looked incredibly uncomfortable, and you could tell he didn't want to say anything. He then looked up and saw my Browns football helmet. He was a fellow football fan, so he began asking me about why I followed that team, my favorite players, etc. In that few minutes of interaction, I could see his guard drop. After a few more minutes of talking about football, we were able to begin speaking about what he came to speak about. I wholeheartedly believe that those personal items helped this man see me as a regular guy who was a husband and dad and as a normal person who also happened to be a pastor. To this day, when I see this man (almost weekly), our conversations still begin with football talk but then turn to deeper conversations, even though they tend to be shorter.

Connecting with the Parents

After you settle in, I would encourage you to connect with parents. In my ministry career, I've found it helpful to call a parents meeting within the first four to six weeks of arriving. Normally I don't believe parents meetings are very effective anymore, especially with how busy our students and their families are today. However, I think this can help set the tone for your relationship with parents. Make it a fun night! Have an ice cream sundae night or a pizza night. Offer some type of food. Have your favorite music on the in the background. Welcome each parent personally and face-to-face as they arrive. Remember, they don't know a lot about you other than what they were told. This little extra piece of personal attention will help them see that you care about them as much as their kids. Make it a very casual night with a small agenda. This will give you a chance to share a little of your vision and plan, but you can also make it a meet-and-greet. What should you communicate that night?

Tell them your story. This is the most important thing you should share—who you are, how you met Jesus, about your family, all the details that let them know who they're trusting their children with.

Show them that you are their ally. I've heard a lot of stories about wedges being driven between youth pastors and parents because youth pastors possibly have taken sides in family matters. As youth leaders/pastors/directors, we absolutely need to be parents' allies. Many of them are already having tough times with these teen years. If they trust their teen to us, they don't need us abusing that trust by forming alliances with their kids. Remind these parents that you're there to serve them as well as their students. Even if you don't agree with the parents' decision, remember that you're not the parent. Do your best to love both sides through tough times and try to stay impartial.

Tell them that you're there to help their kids find out who Jesus wants them to be. Every believing parent deep down wants their children to follow Jesus. I truly believe that. However, I know of some parents who feel inadequate to help their children do that, or because they have multiple children, they feel like they have no time to do that for each child. Reassure them that you're there to help them and their teens find and follow Jesus. While you want to have fun with them and do awesome stuff with them, you're not their entertainment director or summer activities coordinator. You're there to pray for, encourage, challenge, and push each student toward the Savior.

Tell them that you have a plan for the ministry. Take a few minutes to share your ministry vision. This early in a ministry, you may not have a clear vision yet. And that's okay. You just arrived and are still learning the lay of the land. Share with them a little bit of where you think things are going, the vision for ministry God has laid on your heart, and the parts of ministry that you're passionate about. When I arrived at our current ministry, I was up front with our parents about my view of ministry. While I couldn't give them a lot of details on how exactly I would carry out my ministry, I could share with them the vision for student ministry that God had given me. I believe in a discipleship-focused ministry, and we aim to tackle real-life issues head-on in order to help students prepare for life after youth ministry. I was clear that I would not make games a main part of the ministry as other churches did. In my mind, we only had students an hour or two a week, and the last thing they need from us was more entertainment or dollar-store prizes. There was lots of discussion; however, it helped to have that out early on. As we moved forward with that vision, it helped parents, leaders, and new families understand where we were going.

Following that, open up a time for questions and answers. Let parents pepper you with questions and dig into your life a bit. Let them know the person who will be impacting their teens' lives during these critical years.

Connecting with Your Leaders

If you're replacing a former leader, then chances are you will be inheriting a team of volunteers who will be vital in carrying out the vision of the ministry. Before you meet with them, I would encourage you to make sure you have your leader's expectations set. I'd follow the same formula as the one for meeting with parents. Plan a fun night with your leaders! Have them to your house for a BBQ, a bowling night, a beach event, or whatever might be fun in your area! Take them out and just hang with them. Let them see who you are outside of the church walls. Food is always good to have at these events. Break bread with them and just talk. Hear their stories. Learn how they came to that church and why they chose this ministry. Hear their testimony. Have some team-building time with them. What should they know before the night is over?

Tell them your story just as you did with parents. Let them hear how Jesus impacted your life and what He's currently doing in you. This is the most important thing you can share with them. Your story will help them see who you are in Christ. If they see that, it can help tremendously, especially when you don't see eye to eye.

Share your vision. Ultimately you want to create a team that will do ministry and live together. You don't want a businesslike relationship. That doesn't always create a healthy atmosphere. Because these are your frontline players, they'll want to know where you're taking them. Share your heart and share what direction you feel God is leading you to take them.

Reveal your heart. I would encourage every pastor to do this regardless of position. Make sure your team knows that while you're their ministry leader, you're also *their* pastor. Remind them that while there will be trips to take, tasks to be done, and students to deal with, you are also there to serve and lead them as a pastor. They will inevitably have their share of struggles and stress, of personal tragedies and heartbreaks. Remind them that you're there for them as people first.

Share your expectations. In my experience it's extremely healthy to share your expectations early on. As with any company or hierarchy, when the leader changes, people get nervous. People wonder where they stand with the new boss, and they wonder about changes. Having this conversation early does a couple of things. It will help put their minds at ease. Even if they don't understand or agree, at least they know where you're coming from. It will also help them decide if they're in this ministry for the long term. This isn't always a bad thing. Ecclesiastes tells us that there is a time for everything. There are times when leaders might want to move on. You may also feel it's time for a change. It doesn't mean that anyone did anything wrong. It just means a change is needed.

In my first full-time ministry, I didn't do this. I tried to mix myself in with what was going on already. The challenge with that is that the church hired a youth pastor because they felt that it was time to build on what had been going on, not just maintain it. I didn't lay out expectations early, and I didn't take the time to build the team atmosphere. Once I did try to lay these things out a couple of months later, it created a bit of tension and brought up unsettled feelings. This was 100 percent on me; however, I was young and a first-time youth pastor. Additionally, no one gave me a blueprint for this. So in my naivety, I blew it. One couple left the team immediately, which was fine. I believe that they felt it was time to move on for a while, but I could have helped them feel released some time earlier. If a leader feels it's time to move on, then let's help that person find what ministry God *does* have for him or her.

I also believe that student ministry leaders come in all shapes, sizes, and ages. I'd challenge each person reading this. Don't fall into the trap of thinking that you need to find every young adult to build your team. Some churches have a large amount of eighteen- to twenty-five-year-olds, and some don't. I've met many ministries who feel that only eighteen- to twenty-five-year-olds can connect with students. While that's a great age to have for leaders, there are other options as well. When I was in college, I did an internship in New Jersey. There was a leader all of the high school girls adored! They always wanted to see her, hang out with her, and have her come to their plays and games. She had such a sweet and loving heart for them. I learned so much about being Jesus to people by just watching her love them. Her name was Jan. She was much older than them. If I had to guess, I'd say she was in her sixties. The girls loved her so much that they even gave her a shirt that said, "Older than dirt." She was a phenomenal example of not profiling leaders by age. Don't get me wrong. We need youth leaders. We need leaders to mentor and bring up. We need their energy because—well, let's face it—as we get older, it's great to have people to do the running around for us! Those younger leaders connect in unique ways with students. However, let's not cheat our students out of the blessing of having older leaders invest in them, people who have more life experience than even we do, men and women who have the wisdom and stories to help our students learn important life lessons. Be open to talking to anyone who wants to invest their lives in teenagers!

Connecting with the Operations People

There is a team of staff (or volunteers) who are the unsung heroes. They're the operations people. This group of people makes sure the day-to-day operations of the church happen. Many churches have this area structured in different ways, but I'm referring to anyone who isn't a pastoral staff member. This includes the administrative assistants, the custodial crew, the building maintenance team, the outdoor maintenance team, the accounting team, the promotions team, among others. These folks probably do more than we will ever see, and yet they probably get the least amount of appreciation. Spend some time getting to know them, and letting them know you. Each of those teams will interact with your ministry at some point in the course of a normal year. Our relationship with them can either make or break their support of our ministry.

For example, maintaining a good relationship with the custodial team will help when the HS lock-in gets a bit out of hand and isn't cleaned up completely the next morning. You can get a little more leeway when that team knows you and knows that you respect what they do.

Building a relationship with the administrative assistants can get you some help when you're making booklets for a retreat or need flyers printed for the upcoming outreach event. They can save you coming in on your day off.

Connecting with the accounting team will help when you lose receipts from an event. You're trying to schmooze them, but they'll know your heart and character and know that it was an honest mistake.

Many people like to focus on making a good impression on leaders and elders. I say you should make just as much of an effort if not more to make a great impression on the operations teams.

Arriving in a new role is exciting, and it can be nerve-racking at the same time. These are just a few things that I've found helpful to think about as you begin in your new role. I'm sure there will be many more things that you'll run into, and there will always be surprises. In the end, enjoy it!

Conclusion

Ministering to teenagers is one of the most fun, challenging, rewarding, and thankless ministries out there. It definitely is a calling to serve in this ministry.

Over the years I've seen too many young men and women leave ministry early—not always because they feel like they're not called but because they weren't prepared. This has been my concern for years. As each senior class graduates from our ministry, I get to see the next wave of ministers go out to see what God has for them. My heart breaks when I hear that the ministry fire has dimmed a bit after they come back for a visit.

I wrote this book for one reason, namely to help young, up-and-coming potential youth pastors, leaders, directors, and volunteers prepare themselves for what's coming. If we can prep them earlier and better for what they're actually going to face, then maybe we can see youth ministry gain some longevity in each role.

I love student ministry. I think teens are amazing disciples. They're ready for people like you and me to step into their lives and invest into them. They want adults (who aren't their parents) who will not just tell them what to do and how to live but who will walk that path with them. We can't do that unless we are all in. We need to be teachable leaders who accept these roles with the goal of being there for a while. When we came to our current ministry position, I had two daughters who were three and four. Now we have four kids, and the two oldest are ten and twelve. I remember telling the elders when I interviewed that I would love to see my kids graduate from our student ministry. That's my prayer and my hope.

I don't believe in using student ministry as a stepping stone. In fact, I feel like those who do that are insulting those students they're serving. Not that youth pastors won't eventually move onto other roles or that God won't give us new passions for different ministries in the future. However, if we take our first roles with the purpose of waiting for that next opportunity, then we're taking these formative years of our students and wasting them. We need to be all in for as long as the Lord wants us.

Thanks for reading this! I'm praying that my experiences can help others in this journey. I'm not a perfect pastor; however, God has blessed me with a passion for Him and for students, and I pray that what I've learned can be used to help another stick in this wonderfully messy ministry for the long haul!

Thanks for loving students!